Experience Jesus 4

HOW TO ENCOUNTER THE

POWER

OF *God*

DR. PATTY SADALLAH

Experience Jesus 4

HOW TO ENCOUNTER THE

POWER

OF *God*

DR. PATTY SADALLAH

Dedication

To our Sovereign and All-Powerful LORD
who shares His mighty capability and authority with
His faithful servants.

And to all those who say "Yes, Amen, use me!"

Table of Contents

11

Acknowledgments

My sincere thanks go out to the faithful people (too many to name) who participated in the POWER book class. And sincere gratitude for all those who shared their wisdom, and encounter stories in this book: Julie Sordi, George Medellin, Cindy Fiebig, Dianne Wright, Jesse Sliter, Jamael Szucs, Charity Virkler Kayembe, Dr. Mark Virkler, Kim Clement, Stephen Skelton, C.S. Lewis, Brian Green, Robert Henderson, Kenneth Copeland, and Phil Mason. And I would like to thank my faithful weekly prayer partners, Mary Katelyn Grace and Larry Silver along with all of my Spirit Life Circle mentors and members, your support is so important to me.

I would also like to thank Larry Silver for his careful editing, Julie Sordi who made the beautiful lyric video collages for each chapter, and MJ Otto, my wonderful collage photographer. Thank you Matias Baldanza my book cover designer and Daiana Morales, my paperback and e-book formatter. Thank you to Kathy Jiamboi and Kristen Rosenstock from Creative Edge Marketing for the gift of the beautiful series logos.

And appreciation goes to every artist for whom we were blessed by their inspirational songs: Unspoken, Paul Baloche, Dante Bowe, Kalley Heilingenthal, Hillsong United, Amy Grant, Jeremy Camp, Chris Tomlin, Beckah Shae, and Hillsong Worship.

And my husband George and our daughters Jamael, Leah, and Noelle for their constant support. A special thanks to my sister, Michele McLaughlin, who is my biggest fan and gives my books away freely to everyone she meets! And last but by no means least, I would like to thank God for showing up as all these Names so faithfully!

You've Always Been by Unspoken
https://bit.ly/3kCslLp

Experience Jesus
Series Introduction

God's TV Channel

*I*magine that God has His own TV channel. Just like others you might have at your fingertips. But unlike everything on your TV, His is supernatural. When we watch TV, it is a one-directional experience. You can see and emotionally connect with the programming on other channels as a distant observer. But the God channel is a two-way experience. You jump through the television and become part of God's action. This may seem like a strange idea to you, but essentially, this is the experience you will have with this book series. You will learn how to access God through the eyes and ears of your heart to connect with the various Names of Him directly.

> John 10:27 "My sheep hear My voice, and I know them, and they follow Me."

One of the reasons Jesus died for us on the cross was to gain us direct access to the Father so we may know Him intimately one Name at a time.

Colossians 1:9-12 "⁹ For this reason also, since the day we heard of it, we have not ceased to pray for you and to ask that you may be filled with the knowledge of His will in all spiritual wisdom and understanding, ¹⁰so that you will walk in a manner worthy of the LORD, to please Him in all respects, bearing fruit in every good work and increasing in the knowledge of God; ¹¹strengthened with all power, according to His glorious might, for the attaining of all steadfastness and patience; joyously ¹²giving thanks to the Father, who has qualified us to share in the inheritance of the saints in Light."

This book will guide you to experience Jesus yourself. Together, you will address your personal worries, health, family, future, and other life issues. Your experiences with God will move you beyond your limiting beliefs and you will learn how to align yourself with His perfect will for your life.

Why God's Names

The Names of God are personal and powerful. Names like Bridegroom, Mighty Counselor, Friend, Defender, Supernatural Provider, and Healer are intimate for a reason. Would you marry, seek counseling, trust your secrets or your health, lean on in times of crisis someone you can't see, hear, or feel? God was called these Names because He personally showed up for people in these ways in the days of the Bible. He is even more able to do that for you today!

While researching my last book, I was astonished that the original manuscripts of the Bible contain 955 Names of God. This reference will help you see them in their scriptural contexts. https://bit. ly/313CAiR

Unfortunately, in our English Bible translations, we don't see all these distinctive Names because the English language does not have words to make those distinctions. But they exist, in the Greek, Hebrew, Aramaic, and Latin texts.

In Bible times, people encountered God in a variety of different ways and then named Him for those experiences. Here is an example from the Bible when Hagar met God personally and gave Him a Name.

> Genesis 16:11-13 (NOG) [11] Then the Messenger of Yahweh said to her,
> "You are pregnant,
> and you will give birth to a son.
> You will name him Ishmael [God Hears],
> because Yahweh has heard your cry of distress.
> [12] He will be as free and wild as an untamed donkey.
> He will fight with everyone, and everyone will fight with him.
> He will have conflicts with all his relatives." [a]
> [13] Hagar named Yahweh, who had been speaking to her,
> "You Are **El Roi**." She said, "This is the place where I watched the one who watches over me."

The "Messenger of Yahweh" was the pre-incarnate Jesus. Anytime you see the word *"the"* before the word "angel" of the Lord, or in this translation, "messenger," it is referencing the pre-incarnate Jesus. Hagar knew that she was personally encountering God. She named Him *El Roi.* **El** is another word for Yahweh, which means the complete fullness of God. She added the word **Roi** to mean "the God who sees me and watches over me." Hagar had met the Omnipresence of God in a personal way.

It was because she experienced what God did for her that she gave Him this Name. Early in my doctoral journey, the Lord helped me understand more about the importance of encountering God's Names. [i]

Knowing about vs. Knowing[1]

I was meditating on a verse in Titus about the notion of people claiming to know God, but it not showing in their behavior.

> Titus 1:16a, They claim to know God, but by their actions they deny Him.

I asked Jesus to show me the difference between someone who thinks they know You and someone who really knows You. (Note that Jesus' voice will always appear indented and in *italics* so it can be easily identified.)

> *The difference is one knows **about** Me, and the other **knows Me intimately**. Let Me show you what I mean.*

Jesus showed me a man in the desert. He had chapped lips and a distressed look on his face. He frantically looked and thought he saw water. But as he kept walking, he realized that it was only a mirage.

---

1 Excerpt from Just ask Jesus Book 1 Series Introduction of *How to Live a Worry-Free Life* by Dr. Patty Sadallah, pp. 26-28.

Experience Jesus Series Introduction

There was no real water, only something that looked like water. It's good to know what water looks like. It's better to be able to drink some when you are thirsty!

*To learn about Me is like showing a hungry and thirsty man a picture of a magnificent banquet but there is nothing to eat or drink. Seeing the picture may bring some benefits, but he is left ultimately unsatisfied. The actual need is unfulfilled. This is what it is like to only learn **about** Me.*

*The spiritual need to **know** Me is even stronger than that man's physical need for water. A mirage is an illusion; a trick of the eye caused by light refraction and heat waves. Knowing only about Me is a trick too. But it doesn't fool the soul. The soul knows its need for the True God.*

To truly satisfy the hunger and thirst in your soul, you must drink deeply of the Living Water. Water is refreshing, rejuvenating, and restores more than you can see and feel. Come and drink deeply the Living Water. You must eat the food of My Presence. You must enter the Holy of Holies where you can encounter My Presence. I have gained you direct access to the Father by way of the indwelling Holy Spirit by My work on the cross. Do not neglect this privilege.

This is accomplished by you spending time with Me. Consider John 17:3 "This is eternal life, that they may know You, the only true God, and Jesus Christ whom You have sent." To know someone is an intimate thing. To know of something or someone implies knowledge from a distance. It is not My desire for you to know Me distantly or haphazardly in a third-party sort of way as in only through the work of a pastor or a preacher.

You cannot know Me without personally drawing close to Me. It is through steady communion with Me; Father, Son, and Holy Spirit that you will truly Know Me. And knowing leads to trusting, believing, and obeying which are fruits of the eternal life you now have.

It's just like knowing anyone personally. To trust someone, I need to spend time with them to learn who they are and if I can rely on them. After some time, if I feel safe, I tend to want to spend more time and then come to trust them. I spend the most time with people that I like to be around; people who build me up, encourage me, and show me love. No one does that better than You, LORD!"

Yes. The difference between knowing in your head and surrendering in your heart is clarified in James 2:19 'You believe that God is one. You do well; the demons also believe, and shudder.' The demons know who I AM, of course. But they do not accept and surrender to Me and have no intimate relationship with Me. This is an important distinction. Remember, I live in your heart, not in your head.

Yes. LORD. I can see the difference.

Every time you take a drink today, spend time reflecting on the Living Water and come and fellowship with Me. Tune to Me in the quiet and listen for My voice. Seek Me and you will find Me. Spend time getting to know Me. Ask Me to show you things. I certainly have a lot to show you! My heart desires to spend time with you too! Communing with Me is the only way for your spiritual hunger and thirst to be satisfied. This is how you truly know Me!

Encountering the Realness of God

I was listening to the dramatized radio version of C.S. Lewis' *The Screwtape Letters*[ii] by Focus on the Family in my car and came to Letter 31. In this last chapter of the book, the Lord grabbed my attention, and I flushed with Glory bumps.

C.S. Lewis wrote the now-classic *Screwtape Letters* in 1942 amidst WWII. It is a fictionalized story that teaches spiritual warfare in reverse. Screwtape is an experienced demon who is counseling his nephew, Wormwood, a new temper assigned to a "patient," much like a guardian angel for the opposite side. Wormwood's job is to speak lies into his patient's ears to keep him away from God's plans and ensure that he stays well below the calling that God (the Enemy as the demons call Him) has for him.

There are 31 letters that Screwtape writes to Wormwood, and each teaches the lies that the enemy speaks into our lives to throw us off our Christian impact. The entire book and dramatized recording are amazing, but what really got my attention was Letter 31!

Here is a list of quoted snippets from this letter that will hopefully shed light on the relevance of what we are doing here in this book series. Screwtape is looking for Wormwood to take him for his punishment for failing with his patient. He goes on a rant about what Wormwood did that lost this patient to the other side for good:

"All our efforts are dismayed...How well I know the instant that they snatched him from us! Did you see it for yourself? ...There was a sudden change in his eyes as he saw you (Wormwood) for the first time, and he recognized the part you had had in him and knew that you had it no longer! ....It was as if he shed for good the all-wet clinging garments that held him back and was completely cleansed....

He went so easily! It was sheer instantaneous liberation! Did you mark how, as if he was born for it, the little vermin entered the new life? How all his doubts like in the twinkling of an eye became ridiculous!'...

Do you know what your fatal flaw was? When he saw you, he also saw HIM... You allowed him to see that HE is REAL. ... He, to them, is clarity itself. And worse yet, He was in the form of a MAN! The one for whom he thought was dead

23

is ALIVE and even now at his door! ... All our efforts are dismayed!"[2]

Nothing can stop you when you see Him as **real** and for you now. He is at your door. Meet Him, and you will be free, healed, and transformed into the best version of yourself!

Why We Picture Jesus

The three Persons of the Trinity all play a role in the encountering experience. It is ultimately the **Father** who desires that you commune with Him while seeing and speaking with **Jesus** by the power of the **Holy Spirit**. Jesus is the only person of the Trinity that we can honestly imagine. He was a man like us, and that makes Him accessible and understandable as a person. The Father needs the Perfection of Jesus for us to be able to come near to Him. When the Father looks at you, He sees Jesus covering you with His Perfection. The Power to do this is accomplished by the indwelling Holy Spirit, who is God's very essence inside of every believer. This privilege was accomplished by Jesus's work on the cross.

> Genesis 1:1 (NOG) says [1] In the beginning, **Elohim** created heaven and earth. [2] The earth was formless and empty, and darkness covered the deep water. The **Ruach Elohim** was hovering over the water. [3] Then **Elohim** said, "Let there be light!" So there was light.

Elohim is the plural word for a singular God. You see in this verse that the self-existent **Father God** conceives of the Heavens and the Earth. **Jesus, also called the Word**, speaks this conception into existence, and the **Ruach Elohim**, who is the Holy Spirit is the power that manifests it into reality.

---

[2] Focus on the Family Radio Theatre Collector's Edition; The Screwtape Letters by CS Lewis @2009 Tyndale House Publishers. (Snippets from Letter 31)

So, even though you will be connecting with Jesus, know that you are engaging with Elohim, the Triune God. There will be more on how this works in the Creator Chapter of *How to Encounter the POWER of God: Experience Jesus Book 4.*

Jesus Himself instructs us to encounter the Father God by fixing our eyes on Him. He is the relatable third of the Trinity.

> John 14:7-9 [7] If you had [really] known Me, you would also have known My Father. From now on, you know Him and have seen Him."
>
> [8] Philip said to Him, "Lord, show us the Father, and then we will be satisfied." [9] Jesus said to him, "Have I been with you for so long a time, and you do not know Me yet, Philip, nor recognize clearly who I am? Anyone who has seen Me has seen the Father. How can you say, 'Show us the Father?'

Meet God and Get to Know Yourself

Perhaps one of the most important benefits of the *Experience Jesus* series is that you meet your true self in meeting Him. Referencing the Screwtape Letters again, in one of his earliest letters, Screwtape councils Wormwood that God's strategy is to help people realize that He created them uniquely and distinctly. The Devil's strategy is to have people drift away from their uniquely created selves and become like everyone else. Screwtape shares with Wormwood:

> "When He talks of their losing their selves, He only means abandoning the clamor of self-will; once they have done that, He really gives them back all their personality and boasts (I'm afraid, sincerely) that when they are wholly His, they will be more themselves than ever."[3]

---

[3] Focus on the Family Radio Theatre Collector's Edition; The Screwtape Letters by CS Lewis @2009 Tyndale House Publishers. (Snippets from Letter 3)

Consequently, Screwtape continues to advise on how to sweep Christians away with groupthink, popular self-centered notions that lead them farther away from understanding their unique giftings and purposes.

God knows you even better than you know yourself. He truly wants you to see yourself through His eyes. This is part of your journey in this series. As you meet Him and better understand the fullness of His Identity, you meet yourself and discover your Christ Identity, the ideal version of you that He sees you as already.

We can call on God by any of His Names that make Him real to us at the moment and learn directly from Him how to pray with authority for the victories we need in life. Mike Noble from the Cleveland House of Prayer calls God the "trillion-faceted diamond." He often asks people which facet(s) pierced their hearts. Some have met the Provider and can trust Him with their provisional needs but don't know Him as their Friend. Others have met the Great Physician and trust God with their physical needs but not their emotional ones.

Our God is ALL those things and so much more. He wants you to allow more and more facets of the diamond to pierce your heart and transform you. He wants you to be free, whole, and victorious.

> Galatians 5:25 says, "If we live by the Spirit, let us also walk by the Spirit."

It's Normal

God created everyone to see and hear Him with the eyes and ears of their heart. If you were unable to do so, you would never be able to close your eyes and picture a memory or hear in your mind a conversation you had or remember what you heard or saw in a film.

The screen of your mind gives you the ability to see, hear, and feel things. God created the eyes and ears of your heart, most importantly for you to connect with Him. In fact, without the eyes and ears of your heart, you never would have accepted Him as your Savior in the first place. God is not willing for any to perish, so He wired us to be able to communicate with Him.

> 2 Peter 3:9 "The Lord does not delay [as though He were unable to act] and is not slow about His promise, as some count slowness, but is [extraordinarily] patient toward you, not wishing for any to perish but for all to come to repentance."

The entire Bible was written with the same four keys that you will use to encounter God. Two-thirds of the Bible was written through the "ears of the heart" as the human messengers wrote down what they heard straight from the Lord. The other third was written through the "eyes of the heart" as dreams and visions from the Lord were carefully recorded.

God was communicating messages from heaven. He is the same yesterday, today, and forever (Hebrews 13:8). SO, if this is how God spoke to people in the days of the writing of the Bible, He surely can do it now! And even more so now that Christians have the indwelling Holy Spirit whose job it is to fill us with the power to connect with God's Nature and release His Love to others. This direct access to Father God is what Jesus accomplished for us on the cross.

Why the Special Place

In the first encounter that you will have in the next chapter, you will be taken to the **Special Place.** This is for you and Jesus privately. For some, it may be a beautiful location that brings them fond memories of the past. For others, it is a lovely place that they have never seen before. Jesus knows where your special place is, so do not try to figure that out or tell Him where it is. Just let yourself go wherever the Lord takes you.

The special place is essential because once you have seen Jesus there once, you can easily imagine going there again. You can expect to see Him there whenever you need.

He is not limited by this location. When you meet Him there, He can take you anywhere! Some of our encounters will not begin at the special place for specific reasons that will make sense. But I want you to get familiar with having a spiritual home base. Look around, and see more of it as you go back for more experiences. The more you look, the more it will expand.

When I first saw my special place, it was no more than a back porch and a small grassy knoll. It has grown to include a flower path to the sea, a picturesque river and waterfall, a gazebo, a swing set, a dancefloor, and a unique tree. After two years and many adventures with Jesus in my special place, I got to see this place in the natural world in Israel. It was a short walk to the Sea of Galilee! It was incredible. I believe that many places on Earth are shadows of real majestic places in heaven. It was astonishing when I saw the similarities between my photos of that place to the descriptions I had written about it years before!

Jesus can take you anywhere once you begin. Not all your encounters on this journey will start in your special place. However, the more comfortable you are going there, the quicker you can meet Him, even if you are amid chaos or a crisis.

Film Clips, Lyric Videos, and Collages

The Lord is creative. He wants to use as many aspects of the language of the heart to connect with you as possible. God has used media to communicate in each book that He has written through me. This time, the Lord wanted beautiful collages of our chapter lyric videos as a way for you to meditate on the words and connect even more with the songs. Additionally, there are some film clips to reinforce messages and guided imagery audio exercises that help facilitate your encounters. As beautiful as they are in the book, you really must see them in color!

It is amazing to me how much more can be said in a song verse than can be said in pages of a book. The Lord wants you to exercise the eyes and ears of your heart in a variety of ways to strengthen them. Like physical muscles, the more you use them, the stronger they get.

Keep this webpage open so you can simply click on the next media link in the book to watch, listen and experience everything without missing a beat!

Website: www.PattySadallah.com/ExperienceJesus.

God's Heart for You

The capacity to believe in Me is enlarged tremendously by experiencing Me! You encounter the Truth of who I AM to you personally, today, yesterday, and tomorrow when you fix your eyes on Me in all areas. I am sufficient for all of your needs. (see 2 Corinthians 12:9)

When you encounter Me by My Names personally, you begin to collect memories of Me being Who you need for each circumstance. This is how you will live your gospel story in the world and represent Me confidently. The more you encounter Me in these daily, personal ways, the more you give Me access to your heart for transformation.

Every name I have been for others in the Bible, I can be for you. Won't you allow Me to be them for you?

The Gospel is nothing more than a personal recounting of what you have seen, heard, and experienced of God directly. When you encounter Me personally, you are a witness of the REAL God. Memories you collect with Me will increase your trust, faith, belief, and boldness to represent Me well in the world. The more you encounter the different aspects of Me, the more confidence you will have that I AM who I say I AM. The more confidence you have, the more you will inspire others to trust Me. Make them want what you have in Me.

Tell your story. Your story is your living gospel, your record of what I have done in your life. Share every character and aspect of Me you have ever met. Introduce people to Me as the Provider, Healer, Shepherd, Defender, Savior, Counselor, Friend, Way Maker, Creator, etc. so they can know Me likewise.

*I am ready and waiting to meet you in these encounters. I am one God with many facets, way too large for anyone to understand completely. So, meet Me one Name at a time and build memories of personal times when you and I work through challenges and experience joy together. The more you encounter Me, the easier it will be to Trust Me and believe in Me in all areas of life. I Am the **Promise Keeper**. You'll see!*

The Names Addressed in Each Book
Book 1: How to Encounter the *LOVE* of God

1. When you meet the **Heavenly Father,** you are introduced to the power of child-like faith and its mysterious ability to help

you connect with God purely and without the barriers to faith that adulthood brings.

2. When you meet the **Savior**, you learn in a most personal way, why the Lord chose to come as a human and died for YOU. You will understand the price paid for your salvation and why you were worth the cost to God. You will also appreciate the great exchange and the benefits that are yours now and forever as your inheritance.

3. When you meet **Immanuel,** you will encounter the God who always was, is, and always will be with you. He will show you that in an instant, you can see and feel His Covering and connect with His Mind, Will, and Emotion to handle any circumstance your days can bring.

4. When you meet the **Bridegroom,** you will understand the intimacy and value of God's genuine trust and partnership in your life. You will learn the benefits of being united to the All-powerful, All-knowing, All-benevolent, and Ever-Present God.

5. When you meet the **Friend,** you will encounter the joy of God as you have playful adventures with the One you trust with your heart, secrets, and life. You will learn about the powerful favor anointing that comes with the likeability factor of friendship and the role that praise and worship have in it.

Book 2: How to Encounter the *HEALING* of God

1. When you meet the **Great Physician,** He will show you the pathway to vibrant and abundant life. You will learn how to tune in to Him for clarity on all conditions that need to be

met for physical healing and the relationship to spiritual, emotional, and mental health.

2. When you meet the **Comforter,** you will find the way to the peace that surpasses understanding by addressing past heart wounds and allowing Him to help you find forgiveness and give you a new heart.

3. When you meet the **Mighty Counselor,** you will learn how to spot the lies that keep you in bondage and trust God for the Truth that will set you free. Wisdom and understanding are found when you learn how to see your circumstances through God's eyes, ears, mind, and heart.

4. When you meet the **Deliverer,** He will show you the way to find freedom from bondages by standing on His authority and exercising the authority you have by His power to live according to His promises.

5. When you meet the **Miracle Worker,** He will show you key principles for determining His will and accessing His power to pull miracles down from heaven according to His promises.

Book 3: How to Encounter the *DIRECTION* of God

1. When you meet the **Truth,** He will guide you to clarity, wisdom, and understanding by interpreting scripture promises as they relate to your personal calling.

2. When you meet the **Shepherd,** you will see His gentle care, guidance, and protection as you learn to surrender your will and ways to His more perfect plan for you.

3. When you meet the **Author of your Story,** He will show you how to stay aligned with the ideal life plan that He has for you one day at a time.

4. When you meet the **Way Maker,** He will show you how He is working on your behalf often behind the scenes and without your awareness to equip you to accomplish your Kingdom purposes.

5. When you meet the **Supernatural Provider,** He will show you to look beyond natural limitations for accomplishing your work for God. You will encounter His limitlessness and exercise your authority to receive supernatural provisions for your Kingdom purposes.

Book 4: How to Encounter the *POWER* of God

1. When you meet the **Holy Spirit,** you will learn how to tap into the internal power of the Holy Spirit to live your most effective life without fears or limitations.

2. When you meet the **Creator,** you will encounter the complexity and wonder of God and learn about the power of His spoken Word to create. Likewise, how you are made in His image to create as well.

3. When you meet **Almighty God,** you will encounter the Sovereign King of kings and get a greater sense of His Omni-Truths up close and personally. Limiting notions of God will be cast away.

4. When you meet **The God of Justice** you will experience the God of Righteousness who fights on your behalf either on the

spiritual warfare battlefield or in the Courts of Heaven. You will learn how and why you can access the defense of God in your everyday life.

5. When you meet the **Lord of Hosts,** He will show you the angelic realm as its leader and teach you how to cooperate with the ministries of the angels assigned to protect and aid you throughout your life.

The Same Love by Paul Baloche
https://bit.ly/3gR8vtx

How to Encounter God

The conversations and adventures that you will have in this book are real spiritual encounters. They are not figments of your imagination. Believing this is the first step to having meaningful experiences with God.

By way of preparation for this journey, get yourself a journal. It can be as simple as a spiral bound notebook, or as I love to use, one that has Scripture verses at the bottom of every page. I have noticed when I use this kind of journal, that often exactly what Jesus or I am saying on the journal page is reinforced by the Scripture on that page. God is so cool like that!

This is your personal journey. God will call you by name. In fact, He may even give you a new pet name that no one else has ever called you. Stick with this, and I pray that Jesus will meet you one Name at a time exactly where you need Him. I don't know anyone who has encountered the **realness** of Jesus that has not been changed.

If you have not accepted Jesus as your LORD and Savior, this is an important step for you to work through. Appendix B has a special salvation prayer where you can dedicate or re-dedicate your life to

Jesus. We will cover this issue extensively when you meet the Savior in Book 1: Encountering the LOVE of God and He will seal this heart decision for all eternity so you can be assured of your salvation.

Finding God's Channel

The language of the heart is pictures, stories, music, emotions, and metaphors. Jesus demonstrated this by teaching through parables and stories relevant to the culture to connect with the hearts of the people at the time. The language of our heads is analytical and logical. Jesus reflected the character of His Father perfectly using the language of the heart. He spoke in the vernacular of their culture using common images of their day. He does the same thing today as you will see from the experiences that you, and all those for whom God has revealed Himself in this book series. You will learn how to tap into God's channel by putting your brain into the alpha state.

Alpha Brain Waves

Brain waves are measured by frequency, which is cycles per second, or hertz (Hz). They range from very slow to very fast. Alpha waves (8-12 Hz) fit in the middle of the spectrum, between beta and theta waves. Alpha is a state of alert relaxation and fosters creativity. Children from the age of 2 to 8 live primarily in the alpha brain state. They are too young to worry and simply go with the flow of life with play and creative imagination. [4]

Your brain produces alpha waves when you are not concentrating on anything in particular. For example, when you are driving and

---

[4] https://blog.mindvalley.com/science behind-brainwaves/

realize that your mind has been wandering, but you are still able to keep your eyes on the road, you are in alpha.

In the Heavenly Father chapter of Book 1, you realize the importance of approaching God as a child as it naturally connects you with the alpha state and brings the faith of a child. We meet this Name of God first because it is crucial always to meet Him as a child. It took me about two years to realize how important this is to connect with God more effectively.

The alpha brain wave is one of the factors that help you tune into God's channel. You can easily learn the skill of putting your brain in alpha. In fact, the Dialogue Journaling tool we use to encounter God does just that! When your brain is producing these waves as part of your encountering experiences with Jesus, the results can reduce your stress levels and help you feel calmer, more loved, and most importantly, closer to a personal God.

Theta is the brain wave of logical thinking. Most adults spend their waking hours in theta. The brain wave looks more like an active lie detector with fast ups and downs, whereas the alpha state appears as slower rolling hills.

Biblical Meditation

The Bible includes 20 verses to encourage us to meditate on the Word.

> Psalm 104: 34 *May my meditation be pleasing to Him, as I rejoice in the LORD.*

Meditation is a heart posture whereby you surrender all the faculties of your brain to the Lord to gain His wisdom and insight. Wait, doesn't this seem like the stuff that the new agers do? Isn't meditation their word? Sure, but it was God's word first. Do you know why no one counterfeits a three-dollar bill? It is because there is no real $3.00 bill, and it's not a valuable number. The enemy is a counterfeiter. If the new agers are doing it, then something about it is a bit off and was swindled from what is real and valuable.

Let's look at the differences: New Agers seek to connect with the spirit realm when they meditate. They also relax to put their brains into an alpha state. But they seek to connect with spirits in general. We aim to connect with Jesus. This is an important distinction.

> Matthew 7:9-11[9] Or what man is there among you who, if his son asks for bread, will [instead] give him a stone? [10] Or if he asks for a fish, will [instead] give him a snake? [11] If you then, evil (sinful by nature) as you are, know how to give good and advantageous gifts to your children, how much more will your Father who is in heaven [perfect as He is] give what is good and advantageous to those who keep on asking Him.

The Word promises that if you ask for Jesus, you get Jesus. If you ask for generalized spirits, the enemy will surely oblige. Never seek to speak or pray to dead family members or anyone other than God when meditating. The Strong's Exhaustive Concordance defines meditation: "to murmur; to converse with oneself, and hence aloud; speak; talk; babbling; communication; mutter; roar; mourn; a murmuring sound; a musical notation; to study; to ponder; revolve in your mind; imagine; pray; prayer; reflection; devotion.[5] It is a surrender of your entire mind to God's Spirit to meditate on Him. The left-brained activities include reason, written language, and speech. The right-brained activities are related to music, art awareness, intuition, and imagination.

---

[5] https://Biblehub.com/hebrew/yeligch_1897.htm search word Strongs Concordance for "meditation"

You have all these characteristics included if you look at the meditation definition through the filter of all the left- and right activities of the brain.

Dialogue Journaling

We will be using dialogue journaling as our primary tool for connecting with God. Dr. Mark Virkler came up with four simple keys to hearing God's voice[6] for more than 11 years an unrelenting heart desire to commune with God personally. This simple statement summarizes the four keys: Hearing from God is as simple as 1) quieting yourself down, 2) fixing your eyes on Jesus, 3) tuning to spontaneity, and 4) writing it down. These are the steps for what Virkler calls the skill of dialogue journaling or two-way journaing.

1. **Quiet yourself down**- externally and internally

2. **Fix your Eyes on Jesus**- ask and expect to see, hear, and feel from Him

3. **Tune to spontaneity**- allow the pictures, thoughts, and feelings to bubble up without self-effort.

4. **Write down** what you saw, heard, felt, and thought.

The entire Bible was written by God speaking or showing someone something spontaneously and then writing it down so others could read it. Habakkuk 2:1-2 demonstrates these steps beautifully. Habakkuk was a prophet at the time when the Lord was exiling the Jews to other nations for what would be 70 years. The prophet was perplexed by why the Israelites were being taken away and wanted to talk to God about it. The four key steps are revealed in Habakkuk 2:1-2:

---

[6] *4 Keys to Hearing God's Voice* by Drs Mark and Patti Virkler, CWG Ministries

Verse segment/ How it relates to the Four Keys

I will stand on my guard post and station myself on the rampart; / Habakkuk found a quiet place so he could look up to God. He was posturing his heart to speak to God Himself.

And I will keep watch to see what He will speak to me,/

He was looking and listening with an expectation to hear from God personally, using the eyes and ears of his heart.

And how I may reply when I am reproved./ Habakkuk knew it would be a conversation with God. He knew that he could hear what God had to say, AND that he could reply to God.

² Then the LORD answered me and said,/ God did reply personally.

"Record the vision and inscribe it on tablets, so the one who reads it may run."/ God commanded Habakkuk to write down what He was saying. Writing it down is not just for you to remember, but it can also become a blessing for others.

Managing Expectations

Your first exercise will help you with all future exercises. God will take you to your *special place* where you and He will have your first encounter. Your conversations and adventures can begin in this place and Jesus can take you anywhere He wants from there. Getting familiar with your spiritual place will help you comfortably anchor your memories with Jesus. The more you go there, the more He will expand it so you can see and experience more there.

Before we begin, I wanted to manage some expectations. God's voice does not sound like an external, booming, or roaring voice. As we have already learned, it sounds like your own thoughts, pictures, emotions, and songs but is spontaneous with God's character and nature. So, don't jam the receiver with unrealistic expectations that an James Earl Jones-esque voice needs to be speaking in an audible voice for it to be God.

Let's practice using the eyes and ears of the heart right now. Wherever you are, close your eyes. If you are in your bedroom, picture your kitchen or another room in your house. "Look" on the screen of your mind and scan the room. Notice the details that you see. They may not be as clear as if your eyes were open looking at that room, but I'm willing to bet that you have clear impressions in your mind of those rooms. You were just using the eyes of your heart.

Now, close your eyes and begin to sing the Happy Birthday song in your mind. Hear it? That's you using the ears of your heart. If you could hear and see in those quick examples, then you can be sure that you can hear and see Jesus when you ask for Him.

We know that He will show up when you do because He wants to connect with you even more than you want to communicate with Him. God answers yes to heart desires that are in alignment with His will. This means that when you agree to meet with God, He shows up and moves to align you according to His will.

If at first you don't see him in 3D vivid color, that's perfectly OK. You can be grateful with glimpses, sounds, smells, pictures, feelings, or single words initially. Don't allow your expectations to rob you of blessings by dismissing the small beginnings. It will get easier with practice. The more you dialogue journal, the more you will be able to see and hear God.

Hopefully, by the end of this book experience, you and Jesus will be intimate friends and you will be seeing and hearing from Him like a pro. Give yourself some learning curve time. Practice makes perfect. You will meet Jesus in your special place and then He will take the scene where it needs to go.

Encounter Jesus: Your Special Place

Have your notebook or journal handy to record your experience. For many of the encounters in this book series, there will be guided imagery links where you can listen to my voice as a guide. Not every encounter will need this as you get more experienced with your special place. All guided imageries and lyric video links can be found on my website www.PattySadallah.com/ExperienceJesus Keep this page open as you read through the book so those links are handy. They are easily identified by book page number and title.

Special Place Encounter

You can experience this first *special place* encounter by clicking this link http://bit.ly/2g8v8iu. Just relax and listen as I walk you through your first Jesus encounter. Make sure you record what you see and hear Jesus doing with you.

If you do not have a computer, find someone who will talk through these steps for you. It would be too difficult to keep your eyes on Jesus and keep track of these steps as you go. Make sure you keep the experience going long past when the audio instruction has finished. Don't jam the receiver on God just because the audio instruction is complete.

Here are the steps to this encountering experience of meeting Jesus in your special place: Get in a comfortable position where you will not be disturbed. Relax.

- For best results, spend time worshipping and praising Him even before you open in prayer to welcome His presence.

- Begin with a prayer that welcomes God and invites Him to come to speak to you today. You are only wanting to speak to Jesus. Let Him know that He is who you desire to meet with today.

- Let God show you a beautiful place. It could be somewhere you have been before that brings you comfort, or it could be a paradise-like place from your imagination. He knows the place, so just relax.

- With the eyes of your heart, take your time to look carefully on the screen of your mind to the left, to the right, directly in front of you, up above your head, and then down.

- Take in all that you can see, hear, and smell of this place. Awaken all your senses. But don't judge or try harder regarding how much you can see at first.

- After getting a picture in your mind of this place, turn around and see Jesus walking toward you. Don't strain with the eyes of your heart, just relax and allow yourself to see and sense what you can.

- See Jesus come up to you and give you a big loving hug. Feel His embrace. Soak in the feeling of His Presence.

- Sit, lay down, or begin walking with Jesus. Ask Him a question. These questions will change as you work through this book. Your first question is: How do you feel about me, LORD? Tune to flowing pictures, thoughts, and emotions, as these are coming from the Spirit within (Jn. 7:37-39).

- Allow Jesus to completely take over the scene. Watch, listen, and feel what He is doing.

- Write down what you see Him doing, saying, and showing you. Don't question it, just write it down in simple child-like faith.

- Feel free to ask Him another question. Keep the conversation going like you would with a dear friend. The more you do, the more He will show you.

- Let Jesus keep speaking and showing you what He wants until you feel like the conversation has ended.

Give thanks for whatever you got from Jesus. It may be that you could only get a feeling, a small picture, or one word. Anything you receive is a good start.

If you haven't been recording the experience as it is happening, write it down now. Thank God for what He showed you. Consult the Appendix for more tips on Hearing God's voice. You will get more skilled at this as you work through the book.

Each time you encounter God, ask for Him to give you more. If you are seeing pictures, ask Him to explain what they mean. If you hear Him clearly, ask Him for more visions. Remember to thank Him no matter what He gives you!

Champion by Dante Bowe
https://youtu.be/3G_8NiEI3b0

Encountering the POWER of God
Introduction

⚜

*I*n the first book of this Experience Jesus series, you met the loving and tender names of God so you could build a trusting and intimate relationship with Him. Then you met the Healer so He could show you the way to clean up all that distracts you from your purposed destiny. In the third book, you received the clarity of how you fit into God's Kingdom plan, who God sees you as already, and what He wants you to do. In this book you will learn about how big God is and how you can harness the power and authority He has given you to fulfill that plan.

Godly Power and its Relationship to Authority

One of the things I love about our chapter song, *Champion* by Dante Bowe was that it illustrates what it looks like when you are operating with the power and authority that is yours as a child of the Living God.

"You are my Champion
Giants fall when You stand

Undefeated
Every battle You've won
I am who you say I am
You crown me with confidence
I am seated
In the heavenly place
Undefeated
With the One who has conquered it all

When I lift my voice and shout
Every wall comes crashing down
I have the authority
Jesus has given me
When I open up my mouth
Miracles start breaking out
I have the authority
Jesus has given me"[7]

The Greek word for the power that we have in Christ is *dunamus.* It means; the power that comes through God for miraculous force, might, and the ability to perform marvelous works. This word is used 120 times in the New Testament. All power is received by God so *dunamus* is needed for everything you do in life to grow in sanctification and to prepare you for heaven, your eventual glorification.

Related to God Himself, *dunamai* means; I AM the power, I can, I AM able. One of the names we will learn about in this book is Almighty God. If God has all might and power, you can't have any apart from Him. But we know that we can have power through Him because He gives us that authority.

---

[7] https://www.azlyrics.com/lyrics/bethelmusic/champion.html

When we accept the gift of salvation, the Holy Spirit indwells our hearts which grants us the authority to release God's power. One of the reasons that we pray and seal our prayers in the Name of Jesus is because we are claiming the authority given to us by Him. In the Bible story when Peter and John prayed to heal the paralyzed beggar, we see this authority used. (See the entire story in Acts 3:1-18)

> Acts 3:4-9 [4] But Peter, along with John, stared at him intently and said, "Look at us!" [5] And the man *began* to pay attention to them, eagerly expecting to receive something from them. [6] But Peter said, "Silver and gold I do not have; but what I do have I give to you: In the name (authority, power) of Jesus Christ the Nazarene—[begin now to] walk *and* go on walking!" [7] Then he seized the man's right hand with a firm grip and raised him up. And at once his feet and ankles became strong *and* steady, [8] and with a leap, he stood up and *began* to walk; and he went into the temple with them, walking and leaping and praising God.

Interestingly, Peter and John stared at the man intently. What were they doing? They were seeking God to see and hear what He wanted them to do. We learned in the last two books that seeing and hearing in the Spirit and only doing what God reveals is how you pull down manifested miracles. Once they knew exactly what Jesus wanted them to do and say, they prayed it with His authority.

As a child of God, you do not need to come to the Lord as a beggar. You have His authority to agree with what's revealed and speak into reality miraculous things just like Peter and John did.

The Power Source & Releasing the Power

Here is a simple metaphor so that you can understand this relationship. You need electricity to power your house. The power company is the source of that electricity. When you want the lights turned on in your own house, you did not call the electric company and tell them to do that for you. You simply flip a switch, because you have access to that power and the ability to manage it. You simply flip the switch on the wall and the power is accessible and turns on your lights. You are not the source of the power, but you are the one who influences what the power does inside the boundaries of your home.

Understanding Spiritual Realms of Authority

To operate with your power and authority, you must first understand it. There are several reasons why understanding spiritual realms of authority are important.

- It helps to ensure that what you do is within God's anointed boundaries. All things done outside of God's anointing are dead works.

- It helps you respect God's role and responsibility and distinguish it from yours, so you don't get in His way. God will not do your job and you are unqualified to do His job. Yet, this is one of the biggest problems in Christianity today. We unknowingly get in God's way.

- The more you understand the realms of authority, the more you will be able to operate within them for your kingdom purpose.

- The more you understand spiritual realms, the easier it is for you to see the enemy's strategies and address them offensively.

Note the tension in this passage of scripture from 1 Corinthians 2:9-15 that contrasts the difference between those who understand their authority and those who do not.

1 Corinthians 2:9-15 9 but just as it is written [in Scripture],

(Whenever you see all caps in Scripture, it is a direct reference to an Old Testament verse. The below all caps section comes from Isaiah 64:4)

"THINGS WHICH THE EYE HAS NOT SEEN AND THE EAR HAS NOT HEARD, AND WHICH HAVE NOT ENTERED THE HEART OF MAN, ALL THAT GOD HAS PREPARED FOR THOSE WHO LOVE HIM [who hold Him in affectionate reverence, who obey Him, and who gratefully recognize the benefits that He has bestowed]."

¹⁰ For God has unveiled them *and* revealed *them* to us through the [Holy] Spirit; for the Spirit searches all things [diligently], even [sounding and measuring] the [profound] depths of God [the divine counsels and things far beyond human understanding].¹¹ For what person knows the thoughts and motives of a man except the man's spirit within him? So also no one knows the *thoughts* of God except the Spirit of God. ¹² Now we have received, not the spirit of the world, but the [Holy] Spirit who is from God, so that we may know *and* understand the [wonderful] things freely given to us by God. ¹³ We also speak of these things, not in words taught *or* supplied by human wisdom, but in those taught by the Spirit, combining *and* interpreting spiritual *thoughts* with spiritual *words* [for those being guided by the Holy Spirit].

¹⁴ But the natural [unbelieving] man does not accept the things [the teachings and revelations] of the Spirit of God, for they are foolishness [absurd and illogical] to him; and he is incapable of understanding them, because they are spiritually discerned *and* appreciated, [and he is unqualified to judge spiritual matters]. ¹⁵ But the spiritual man [the spiritually mature Christian] judges all things [questions, examines, and applies what the Holy Spirit reveals], yet is himself judged by no one [the unbeliever cannot judge and understand the believer's spiritual nature].

These verses clarify that we live in the new covenant days where the Lord has given us the ability to know Him intimately. Praise God that you live in this generation and have this access and authority!

The Goals of this Book:

- To Expand your understanding of how BIG God IS.

- To understand the relationship between the earthly and spiritual realms.

- To understand God's authority and your authority as a citizen of heaven.

- To understand how you as a born-again believer can operate and cooperate with God's spiritual realm here on earth now.

We will use these goals as guides for each of our Names of God explorations and encounters.

Levels of God's Presence

To be trusted to release God's power by His authority, you must have the experience of His Presence and the grounding of the Truth of the Word of God. It is this intimacy that builds the trust required to release God's love and light. It is important to remember that we need to want His presence more than His power. To seek His power over His presence is to have the wrong heart motivation. Experience God's nearness for yourself to learn the depths of this truth. I remember Tommy Tenney writing in his book *God Chasers*: "Intimacy will bring about "blessing" but, the pursuit of "blessing" won't bring about intimacy." Keep your eyes fixed on Jesus alone, not on outcomes or what you want Him to DO for you. Just BEING with HIM will cause blessings to happen for you.

To this point, I asked the Lord; what more do You want to say or show me about your Presence? Below is the conversation I had with God about it.

The Lord showed me a gentle sprinkler, then a power washer, then a tidal wave. What do these things mean Lord?

Your physical body cannot handle the full measure of My presence. I give you a taste, a glimpse of who I AM little by little as you spend time with Me in the Word, prayer, and communion. This is like the sprinkler. It is refreshing and edifying. The power washer represents when you can handle more and more of My powerful presence and glory. I begin to equip you for greater measures of anointing. Your impact and influence grow with an increasing measure of My presence.

2 Corinthians 3:18 And we all, with unveiled face, continually seeing as in a mirror the glory of the Lord, are progressively being transformed into His image from [one degree of] glory to [even more] glory, which comes from the Lord, [who is] the Spirit.

The tidal wave represents the highest level of My presence that only your new heavenly body will be able to handle. This new body will be able to handle an eternity of My presence. That level would certainly kill anyone in a human body.

WOW. That is super cool, Lord. Thank you for the way you help me grow in the levels of your presence. You continue to give me more and more experiences and encounters with You that show me who You are Lord and I appreciate the metaphor that You will continue to increase that power and level of Your presence as I can handle it. Power washers are effective to clean dirty things too.

Yes. Exactly. As you encounter Me, you will want to clean up more and more in your life. As you shed these areas and clean them up, you become more equipped to handle the things I have for you to do, teach, write, speak, etc.

Thank you, Lord. I receive it and am grateful and honored to receive your Presence!

As you learn these new things about God's power and your authority, and as you see His face for an increased anointing, you will grow in wisdom and authority and will become more equipped to release God's love and power in increasing levels.

Ephesians 1:13-14 [13] In Him, you also, when you heard the word of truth, the good news of your salvation, and [as a result] believed in Him, were stamped with the seal of the promised Holy Spirit [the One promised by Christ] as owned *and* protected [by God]. [14] The Spirit is the [a]guarantee [the first installment, the pledge, a foretaste] of our inheritance until the redemption of *God's own* [purchased] possession [His believers], to the praise of His glory.

This verse reveals God's promise of the seal of the Holy Spirit. This ensures our increasing capability to grow in levels of anointing. This promise confirms that believers are stamped and sealed as a child of God.

Once sealed, this verse shows the progression toward our maturity in Christ. Notice that we need to continually see God. Fixing our eyes on Him is the way we grow from glory to glory. Where there is God's presence there is His glory and where there is His glory, there is His transformational anointing.

The Relationship Between Spiritual and Earthly Realms.

This amazing metaphor was given to Cindy Fiebig in December 2019. Cindy is a member of my Spirit Life Circle. She wanted a greater understanding of the spirit realm as it related to our earthly realm. The Lord gave her this incredible Star Trek-inspired metaphor.

For those who are not familiar with the Star Trek Holodeck, it is a virtual reality simulator program that allowed people on the spaceship Enterprise to experience anything virtually. It was often used for training purposes to prepare people for dangerous scenarios and was even used for entertainment purposes.

The Lord used this metaphor to compare and contrast the natural and spiritual realms.

Holodeck and Enterprise	Natural world and Spirit realm
The holodeck is made up of energy that is transformed into matter that is perceivable by the senses, and there is the awareness of the passage of time.	God created everything in the natural world from light to energy. He caused all matter to materialize from this original energy. It is perceivable by the senses, and there is the awareness of the passage of time.
It seems like the real world when people where in it, but it exists *inside* the Enterprise, which is the true reality.	The spirit dimension surrounds, undergirds, and interpenetrates the natural dimension. The natural dimension is a subsystem *within* the spiritual dimension.
The ship is on the outside, surrounding the holodeck.	I can picture Jesus as greater than the universe, and I sense Him above me and surrounding this place.

The computer can insert or transform holodeck matter instantly.	Power from the spirit can transform (heal) or create something (miracle) in this natural world instantly.
Everything in the holodeck disappears when the computer is commanded to "end the program."	One day, at God's command, the present heaven and earth will be gone and transformed into a new heaven and new earth. Matthew 24:35 Heaven and earth [as now known] will pass away, but My words will not pass away.
When the captain wants to reach someone in the holodeck, s/he uses the com badge. Every crew member has one and they wear them while inside the holodeck.	The voice of the Holy Spirit is like my "com badge." I can clearly hear Him speaking to me from the spirit. I can also see images and sense emotions from the spirit realm.
People outside of the holodeck can enter it. Sometimes they disguise themselves as holodeck characters.	Angels enter the natural world, often disguised as people.
The holodeck is operated primarily by voice command.	God's word creates and directs this natural world. I believe, therefore, I speak. I create when I speak.
To the characters, the Enterprise is real.	The spirit realm is real – in a sense, far more real than the natural world. I can see it. I believe in it. I know it is true.

You are a Citizen of Heaven?

A citizen is a person who legally belongs to a kingdom or nation and is entitled to the rights and protection of that place. A citizen adopts cultural practices and abides by the laws of that nation or kingdom.

All born-again believers are citizens of heaven. There are three stages or steps to your walking in that citizenship.

1. Understand that you are a citizen of heaven and that citizenship overrides your earthly citizenship.

   Philippians 3:18-20 [18] For there are many, of whom I have often told you, and now tell you even with tears, who live as enemies of the cross of Christ [rejecting and opposing His way of salvation], [19] whose fate is destruction, whose god is *their* belly [their worldly appetite, their sensuality, their vanity], and *whose* glory is in their shame—who focus their mind on earthly *and* temporal things. [20] But [we are different, because] our citizenship is in heaven. And from there we eagerly await [the coming of] the Savior, the Lord Jesus Christ;

2. Because you are a citizen of heaven, you should be different. Your citizenship should be distinguishable.

   Romans 12:1-2[1] [a]Therefore I urge you, [b]brothers and sisters, by the mercies of God, to present your bodies [dedicating all of yourselves, set apart] as a living sacrifice, holy and well-pleasing to God, *which is* your rational (logical, intelligent) act of worship. [2] And do not be conformed to this world [any longer with its superficial values and customs], but be [c]transformed *and* progressively changed [as you mature spiritually] by the renewing of your mind [focusing on godly values and ethical attitudes], so that you may prove [for yourselves] what the will of God is, that which is good and acceptable and perfect [in His plan and purpose for you].

3. Your life should be proof or evidence of your heavenly citizenship. Your life will reveal the difference. The entire chapter of Hebrews 11 shows us the stories of faithful servants that lived lives of great faith and dedication. They kept their eyes on the promises beyond this natural world. This small section is speaking of Abraham's faith.

Hebrews 11:9-10 [9] By faith he lived as a foreigner in the promised land, as in a strange *land*, living in tents [as nomads] with Isaac and Jacob, who were fellow heirs of the same promise. [10] For he was [waiting expectantly and confidently] looking forward to the city which has foundations, [an eternal, heavenly city] whose architect and builder is God.

The Fluency of the Language of the Heart

The Lord speaks to you using the language of the heart which includes spontaneous pictures, stories, emotions, music, thoughts, feelings, and sensations. It is important to note that it is called the language of the heart because it is not your body or brain that is engaging with the Lord when you receive or even speak this language back to God. It is the spirit part of you, not the physical part of you that engages with God. Don't get in God's way by thinking that you need to be smart enough to receive or understand this language, It has nothing to do with your brain. Your spirit is connecting with God's Spirit when you encounter God.

The easiest way to learn any language is with immersion. I liked the thesaurus.com search results for this word.

immersion ◀◻ ☆   SEE DEFINITION OF *immersion*

noun **absorption**

OTHER WORDS FOR *immersion*

captivation	engrossment	hang-up	involvement	prepossession
concentration	enthrallment	holding	occupation	raptness
engagement	fascination	intentness	preoccupation	

TRY *immersion* IN A SENTENCE BELOW ↓   ▣ MOST RELEVANT

8

Becoming immersed in something does appear to require quite a lot of focus based on these synonyms. Living in a country, for example, is the easiest way to pick up its native language. It is much less effort than studying sentence structure in a classroom which is just engaging your brain and not your other senses. Immersing yourself in encounters and experiences in a cultural context engages all of your senses and gives you live context for what the words mean.

When our daughter Noelle was four years old, our family went on a ski vacation in Montreal and Quebec, Canada. We were immersed in a French-speaking culture for 10 days. People spoke to us all day in French and even the television cartoons were only in French. Noelle was able to understand and began speaking French with this short exposure to the language and experience! We were astonished at how quickly she was able to understand and speak it!

Likewise, *living* with the Lord is the easiest and quickest way to know His language too. Simply *being* with the Lord frequently will increase your fluency in recognizing all the many ways He communicates.

---

[8] https://www.thesaurus.com/browse/immersion?s=t

Switches

When you are connecting with God using the language of the heart, you are meeting Him where He is and seeing, feeling, thinking, and sensing things from His perspective. One of the ways to know if you are connecting with God is to recognize when you are not. Knowing when He somehow feels distant, or that you are failing to properly reflect His love are examples of this.

The Lord coined the phrase "switches" for me in recent months referring to times when you know you need to switch from your perspective to His. Let's look at examples of some switches.

1. Be honest with yourself and God.- When God feels distant it is more because of you than Him. God's word promises that He never leaves or forsakes you. God knows everything anyway, so you might as well have an openhearted posture and be real with Him. Even when you are mad at God, He appreciates addressing it with Him. He will not fall off his throne. So, the first switch is to ask yourself, how am I distancing God? Confess and repent for whatever bubbles up and fix your eyes back on God.

2. Speak Scripture out loud. Speaking scriptures activates the sword of the Spirit which immediately brings God into your presence.

3. Worship by praising God and speaking or singing in tongues. Exercising the gift of tongues cooperates with the Holy Spirit. Surrendering your mouth allows Him to pray perfect prayers over you, while you offer perfect worship to Him. And worship opens the gates of God's presence.

4. Call upon God's names. God's names have His power. This is why we pray in Jesus's name. Simply saying any of the names of God is an invitation for that aspect of God to come to your aid.

5. Take a break. Striving in your strength is the wrong heart posture to hear from God. Taking a walk in nature and just enjoying God's creation without thinking about connecting with God will relax your heart and the Lord is more easily able to connect with you.

6. Breathing deeply slows down your heart rate and relaxes you. Breathe in the power of the Holy Spirit and breathe out stress and anxiety. Breathe in speaking the Bible truths related to God's names, character, and promises. Breathe out the opposite of those things, lies that are keeping you in fear and anxiety.

7. See Him. Visualization is a powerful intervention because you will remember more about what you experienced with Jesus than you would about what He says alone. Strengthen your capacity to see Him by practicing looking for and engaging with Him in your special place.

8. The word promises that if you seek the higher gifts, He will answer that prayer. Ask him for an increase in the fluency of the language of the heart. And remember to immerse yourself, prioritizing time with Him and in the Word as sacred holy habits.

The Names you will Meet:

For each name we explore in this book, we will look at God's power, and your power, and how to connect the two in cooperation for God's will to be done.

The Holy Spirit- You will learn about the third person of the Trinity. What He does, how to sense Him, and how to cooperate with Him.

The Creator- Science is simply us trying to understand God's world. Science and God are not at odds. We will learn how amazing our Creator is, how He creates, and how we create as well by His power.

Almighty God- You will have a deeper appreciation of the greatness of the King of kings, and Lord of lords. You will learn about God's reigning authority and the power you have as well as a child of God.

The God of Justice- God promises to fight your battles. You will learn the rules of the spiritual realm, how to work within them and exercise your authority to call upon the Defender to implement justice.

The Lord of Hosts- The ministry of the Angels is under the authority of Jesus, the Lord of Hosts. Here you will learn about the ministry of angels and the spiritual realm of the evil principalities. How to cooperate and empower angels by your authority as a child of God.

Introduction to the POWER Book Encounters:

Remember to meet the Lord as a child and allow Him to direct the encounters. Also, beginning each encounter with doing something fun with the Lord is always a great heart-posturing exercise.

1. Lord, how have I made you too small? Highlight an area in my life where I need to know that you are bigger than I realize.

2. Lord, show me what I/ (it) will look like when I can handle more of your presence. What will prepare me for that upgrade?

3. Lord, how can I become more fluent in the language of the heart so I can connect with You more easily and trust that I can exercise my authority in You?

4. Lord, help me better understand what It means that I am a citizen of heaven, and how I can live out the truth of this citizenship here on earth.

Spirit Move by Kalley Heilingenthal
https://youtu.be/tbdSQ8MLnYs

Meet the Holy Spirit

The Holy Spirit is the least understood member of the Trinity of God. The word trinity is not in the bible. But the truth and evidence of the Trinity are quite evident throughout the Bible when you know how to see it. God is ONE God within three persons, or three unified as One.

To begin to understand the Holy Spirit, it helps to understand how He fits in the Godhead of the Trinity.

God is One Being

A being is the qualities and essence of WHAT you are. A Person is the uniqueness of WHO you are. God is One in Being as Three Persons. The Father, Son, and Holy Spirit are all separate Persons of the Being of the ONE True God, existing in perfect unity. All three share what I have called in the past the ISNESS of God. The attributes of God include His four Omni-Characteristics of Omnipotence, Omniscience, Omnipresence, and Omnibenevolence. That is all strength, wisdom, timeless presence, and love.

Genesis 1:1 (NOG) In the beginning **Elohim** created heavens and earth.

Elohim is a plural name word for a singular God. Let's look at how all three persons of the Trinity had a role or a distinctive part to play in Creation.

Genesis 1:26 26 Then God said, "Let *Us* (Father, Son, Holy Spirit) make man in Our image, according to Our likeness [not physical, but a spiritual personality and moral likeness]; and let them have complete authority over the fish of the sea, the birds of the air, the cattle, and over the entire earth, and over everything that creeps and crawls on the earth."

God is Three Persons

The Heavenly Father is the container of the Will of God. He conceived of Creation. He desired it. He imagined it. He conceived of it, and He willed it into existence.

Now let's look at the Son of God. One of the Names of Jesus is the Word and another is the Way. John 1:1-3 John shows us that Jesus is the Word.

John 1:1-3 In the beginning the Word already existed. The Word was with God, and the Word was God. ² He was already with God in the beginning. ³ Everything came into existence through him. Not one thing that exists was made without him.

So we see here that Jesus spoke the WORD that the Father Imagined. All creation happens because of the Spoken Word. Jesus is also the WAY.

John 14:6 *Jesus* answered him, "I am the way, the truth, and the life. No one goes to the Father except through me

68

So Jesus is the Way or the method to salvation.

The Holy Spirit is the Spirit of God. He is also the person whose job is to be the conduit of the supernatural power of God. He is the one that manifests the spoken word of Jesus according to the will of the Father. It is far easier for us to image the Holy Spirit as a "force" because of His job, but He is no less of a person.

So the Father is the holder of the Will, Son speaks and does only what He sees and Hears the father commanding, (see John 5:19) and the Holy Spirit releases the power to make happen the expressed will of the Father and the spoken commands of the Son. They act in perfect sync as three distinctive persons of One God.

Each person of the Godhead has a specific role to play. The Heavenly Father is the keeper of the will of God. He holds the Kingdom's plan and intentions. Jesus is the Word and the and the Way. The Holy Spirit is the power to make God's will manifest through Jesus.

The Holy Spirit shares the divine personality, including the fullness of the character of God. The Holy Spirit is described in the Word as the living water, as the mighty blowing wind, and as the refiner's fire. He is the energizing power of God. It's hard to picture all of that as a person. Yet, He is a person. When you experience God in any of the ways we teach you are encountering the Trinity through the power released by the Holy Spirit.

The Father doesn't need you to do His job, and the Son doesn't need you to do His job, but the Holy Spirit is here for you and requires your cooperation to do His job.

1 John 2:27 [16] And I will ask the Father, and He will give you another [a]Helper (Comforter, Advocate, Intercessor— Counselor, Strengthener, Standby), to be with you forever—

69

[17] the Spirit of Truth, whom the world cannot receive [and take to its heart] because it does not see Him or know Him, *but* you know Him because He (the Holy Spirit) remains with you *continually* and will be in you.

The Holy Spirit is your Comforter, Mighty Counselor, Helper, Advocate, Teacher, and Strength. He is the power of the fullness of God within you. This means you have access to the Omni-Truths of God within you. He guides you to transform into your Christ-Identity, so you may align yourself with the will of God.

Two distinctive baptisms happen with the Holy Spirit. The first is the baptism of salvation when you receive the Holy Spirit as a seed in your heart. Seeds contain the full capability of the intention of their design. And require the proper atmospheric conditions to grow into their full fruit-bearing purpose.

Acts 2:38 [38] And Peter said to them, "Repent [change your old way of thinking, turn from your sinful ways, accept and follow Jesus as the Messiah] and be baptized, each of you, in the name of Jesus Christ because of the forgiveness of your sins; and you will receive the gift of the Holy Spirit.

A Spiritual baptism happens when you surrender your will to the Lord in salvation. A seed of the Holy Spirit is deposited in your heart at that moment. Like any seed, it contains the full capability to grow to complete fruitfulness. But at this point, the seed is just the seed. It can lay dormant in the heart of the believer for an entire life if not activated. Part of salvation is making a public declaration of your surrender to the Lord. This is the reason why Jesus allowed John the Baptist to baptize Him. The word commands us to be baptized by water. But that outward symbol is not required for the baptism of salvation to occur. This is a spiritual transaction that occurs in the believer's heart when they surrender their lives to Jesus Christ.

The second is the baptism of the Holy Spirit which causes Him to become activated in your heart.

We learn about the baptism of the Holy Spirit in Acts. Jesus promised to send the Helper after He ascended to heaven. In this way, God's personality, nature and character, and power can be multiplied by all the believers in Christ.

> Acts 2:4 [4]And they were all filled [that is, diffused throughout their being] with the Holy Spirit and began to speak in other [a]tongues (different languages), as the Spirit was giving them the ability to speak out [clearly and appropriately].

Receiving the baptism of the Holy Spirit activates the spirit to a deeper dimension. The evidence shown in this first outpouring of the Spirit was demonstrated by the gift of tongues. This is just one of the nine manifestation gifts of the Holy Spirit. It is not the only evidence of the baptism of the Holy Spirit. I think the Lord chose this one though to prove that people were surrendered to God at that moment. To speak in tongues is to cooperate with the Holy Spirit by allowing Him to give the words while you surrender your tongue and make the utterance.

How the Holy Spirit Communicates with You

Just like God is one God with three persons, we are one person with three parts. We are body, soul, and spirit.

- **Body-** Your body is the external layer and is created to exist in the physical world. It houses the five senses of the physical body: seeing, hearing, smelling, touching, and tasting, It does not go beyond the physical world.

- **Soul-** The soul is your life essence. It's a core part of you that stays alive when you die. It houses your mind, will, and emotions at the very basic level. It abides, which means to continue to your eternal destination at death. So it was created for both heaven and earth.

- **Spirit-** The spirit was created to communicate with God. It is the power of your life. It is your primary connection to the Holy Spirit and spiritual realms. It houses your spiritual senses of the inner man: the eyes and ears of your heart as well as sensing, smelling, and tasting in the spirit. Once saved, the Holy Spirit can lead you to connect with God's mind, will, and emotions. So you can align your heart and will with His.

Everyone was born with senses of the heart, that is the ability to connect with God. But only born-again, believers have the privilege of the indwelling Holy Spirit which allows you to connect with God's mind will, and emotion.

How to Sense the Holy Spirit Within

In his book *How to Walk by the Spirit*, Dr. Mark Virkler included this diagram below to help understand the relationship between these senses.[9] The Lord helped me to understand this.

If you notice the diagram, My senses are on the inside of the pentagon sections and yours are on the outside circle. Imagine doors that can either open or close passageways from the pentagon sections to your outer circle. A closed door would block Me from influencing you. An open door would allow Me to transform you. For Me to shine through you, you need to open the doors. Surrendering your senses to Me opens the doors so My best can shine through you.

---

[9] *How to Walk by the Spirit* By Drs. Mark and Patti Virkler, Lamad Publishing, 2007. Diagram page 77.

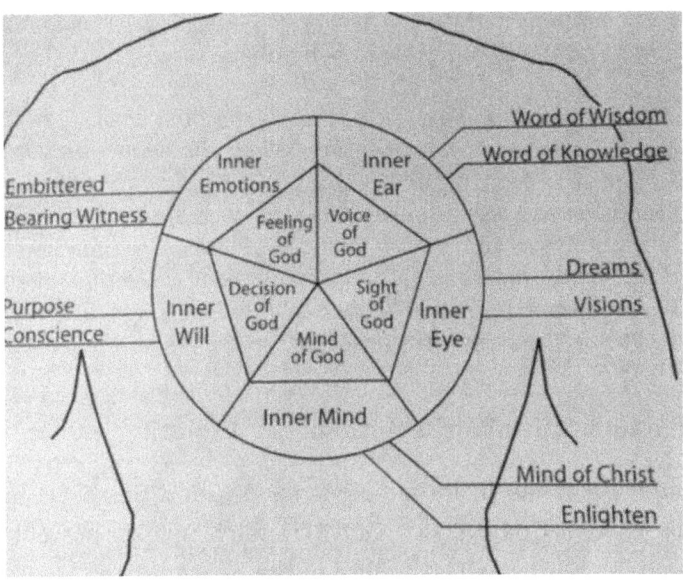

Wholeheartedness is being in touch with all of the spiritual senses of your inner man. Many times you are more in touch with your own will and emotions more than you are with Mine. When you focus on yourself, you miss the blessings I have for you. I don't want you to miss a single best blessing. There are always silver linings in your challenges. I want you to see what they are. So, ask, seek, and knock and I will reveal them to you.

Matthew 7:7 **7** "[a]Ask and keep on asking and it will be given to you; seek and keep on seeking and you will find; knock and keep on knocking and the door will be opened to you.

Increasing your sensitivity to what is influencing your spirit is the key. When you're able to step back, observe and ask, what is causing this feeling or emotion? Then asked Me for insight, I can revive, restore. lift and cover you whenever negative influences try to affect you. Recognize when these senses are not from Me. Don't be left off guard when you see your emotions getting the best of you. Pause, then bring Me into focus. It will help you every time!

When your heart joins with Mine we become one. There is much more power in that fusion. When you cooperate with Me for your best, we can become a dynamic duo! Get in a group. Pray together for wisdom and understanding of how to grow Me in your heart faster. When you pray for these things alone that's great. But when you pray with others then I am multiplied. You can receive 100-fold blessings and send 10,000 to flight. (See Joshua 23:10)

How the Holy Spirit Works through the Anointing

The anointing is the material substance of God's presence. It is the tangible power of God that gives God's chosen people the power to fulfill God's call in their lives. The anointing can be stored and transmitted. The Lord gave me this metaphor to help us understand it.

Do you remember sea monkeys when you were a child? They were those little capsule toys that started out looking like tiny pills and the longer they stayed in the water, the bigger they grew they took shape as tiny living creatures. The anointing is like that. You receive a small seed of the Holy Spirit when you accept Me as Lord and Savior. It could sit as a tiny seed, lying dormant with full capability. Or it could grow when immersed in the Living Water. The more you abide, trust, love, worship, and follow Me, the more your anointing grows and takes form. As it grows, it changes your heart, giving you the power and wisdom to do My will so that you can pass it on.

Understanding the Anointing

The Hebrew word for anointing is *mischchah* which means "smearing". The Greek word for it is *chrisma* which translates to "rubbing in". The material substance of the anointing gets rubbed into you. The more time you spend with God the more anointing will stay with you.

The power of the anointing is tangible. It is felt to the touch and can be transmitted from one person to the next. The power can be stored like the battery on fabrics and liquids. The Lord explained it this way;

> *Memory foam receives an imprint when touched and then pops back after you take your hands off of it. But when that happens over and over and over and over, the imprint remains. Evidence of it remains visible after the person gets up. The same is true when My anointing is present repeatedly in your life. This is accomplished by a lifestyle of abiding in My presence.*
>
> *The more you boldly wear Me for all to see, the more the rubbing of the anointing will dry permanently like an indelible tattoo. People will "feel" Me when they are near you. They will have a sense of Me because of your boldness.*
>
> *Elisha's bones were so steeped by My presence that every atom and neuron of his body was saturated by My anointing. The anointing remained on the prophet's bones because of His boldness for Me. It was a permanent imprint. Elisha's bones carried so much anointing that a dead body came back to life when it touched his dry bones. (See 2 Kings 12:)*

What does the Anointing Feel Like?

The anointing is perceivable by your senses. Jesus felt the anointing leaving his body when the woman with the issue of blood touched his robe. (See Mark 5:30), I often feel glory bumps (goosebumps) when I'm praising and worshiping the Lord. Or when I'm sharing God with other people.

You can grow in your sensitivity to perceiving the tangible anointing. The more awareness you have of the anointing the more able you are to yield to the Holy Spirit's guidance and cooperate with Him for it.

The anointing is felt in a variety of ways and is often different depending on the kind of anointing you're experiencing. Here's a list of some of the ways the anointing was sensed by prophets in the Bible.

- Jeremiah described it as a burning in the mouth. I believe what he means here is that God gives him the urgency of words to speak. (See Jeremiah 5:14)

- Daniel described it as shaking or trembling (See Daniel 10:10-11)

- Ezekiel describes the feeling of an out-of-body experience or a weightlessness and sometimes a pushing forward like God's hand on your back, (See Ezekiel 3:14)

- Samuel described the enlightening of the word of God where he was aware that God was giving him understanding and wisdom. (See 1 Samuel; 3:21)

- Luke described it as a passion or thrill or excitement when he could feel the spirit leading him into understanding. (See Luke 24:32)

I have also experienced it as the sensation of warm liquid flowing through my body, and also falling backward or falling forward. To be slain in the spirit is to lose physical consciousness while having a visionary encounter with God. When I asked the Lord what He wanted us to know and do about the anointing, He answered:

I want you to become super sensitive to the feelings and sensations of the different types of anointing so you can recognize what I'm doing and what I want to do through you. The first step is to desire more anointing power and then ask Me for a greater level of sensitivity. When you are tuned to Me in that way, you will not miss the small nudges and unctions that direct you to do or say something. To be a guide you must be an expert in the terrain. So remember to stay focused on Me. Ask for the increase and be sensitive to the feelings of the anointing. Be obedient to My promptings. Stay in the Word, pray in tongues every day – it feeds Me and blesses you. Then you will see an increase in the anointing.

God gave some specific instructions in this last journal entry. He is saying to first pay attention so you know when you are receiving the manifestation of the anointing. And He's saying that there's always a purpose for it, so make sure you ask Him to clarify its purpose. Next, realize that He wants to release it. So learning how to channel the anointing according to God's purposes is important.

Three Major Types of Anointing

The Believers Anointing- This anointing is only for new covenant believers. It did not exist in the Old Testament days. It is the anointing within your heart because of the indwelling Holy Spirit. As already explained above, it is activated at the baptism of the Holy Spirit.

You can grow your believer's anointing by increasing your quality time with God. This leads to a rise in God's empowering grace, inviting God's glory. So we can see that the believers anointing which we received at salvation and activated at the baptism of the Holy Spirit can be increased as we mature in Christ.

The Ministerial Anointing- This is the anointing upon a person given when the Lord has a specific assignment for them. It is also known as the anointing upon. This was the anointing that the Old Testament prophets operated under when God would give them an assignment. God's power would come upon them to say and do what was needed at that moment. Today it works in concert with the believers anointing. This anointing is activated when God adds the manifestation gifts of the Holy Spirit to the ministerial gifts needed for a specific purpose at the moment they are needed.

> Romans 12:6 ⁶ Since we have gifts that differ according to the grace given to us, *each of us is to use them accordingly*: if [someone has the gift of] prophecy, [let him speak a new message from God to His people] in proportion to the faith *possessed*;

In the Encountering the DIRECTION of God book, we covered the nine manifestation gifts of the Holy Spirit, as well as the ministerial and motivational gifts in great detail. The nine manifestation gifts of the Holy Spirit are released when the Holy Spirit determines they are needed and when a person has proven themselves trustworthy to release them. They are:

- **Speaking in unknown tongues** (See 1 Corinthians 14:27) This type of tongue is for the releasing of a blessing to others. This is where a person can miraculously speak in other actual languages, that they could not speak before. So the hearer of that language can understand the gospel. This is distinguished from the heavenly language that believers pray in their own unknowable language to connect with God.

  1 Corinthians 14:27 If anyone speaks in a tongue, it should be limited to two or at the most three, and each one speaking in turn, and one must interpret [what is said].

- **Interpretation of Unknown Tongues** (See 1 Corinthians 14:27) This is for public situations primarily because the hearer needs to receive in their own language. One can also ask for wisdom and understanding about what they are praying when speaking in the second type of tongues.

- **Prophecy** Speaking and sharing what God has given to you to share. Sometimes about future needs and can be warnings for repentance. But it will always be given to encourage, exhort and uplift and direct.

  Revelation 19:10b For the testimony of Jesus is the spirit of prophecy [His life and teaching are the heart of prophecy]."

- **Word of Knowledge** When the Lord shares something about someone or something that you shouldn't have the ability to know so you can know how to pray for them or the circumstance. Jesus demonstrates this in John 14:18 when Jesus spoke with the woman at the well.

  John 14:18 18 The fact is, you have had five husbands, and the man you now have is not your husband. What you have just said is quite true."

- **Word of Wisdom** when the Spirit speaks clarity about a scripture, an event, or gives direction.

  Acts 11:28 **One of them named Agabus stood up and prophesied through the [Holy] Spirit that a severe famine would come on the [a]entire world. And this did** happen during the reign of [b]Claudius.

- **Discernment of spirits** When the Lord helps you understand the truth from lies. Knowing which spirit is influencing you or others.

  Acts 27:23-24 23 For this very night an angel of the God to whom I belong and whom I serve stood before me, 24 and said, 'Stop being afraid, Paul. You must stand before Caesar; and behold, God has given you [the lives of] all those who are sailing with you.'

- **Faith** The supernatural ability to believe God for His promises so you can stand on them. It is given at the time and for the circumstance for which it is needed.

Hebrews 11:33 (speaking of behaviors lived by heroes of the faith) 33 who by faith [that is, with an enduring trust in God and His promises] subdued kingdoms, administered justice, obtained promised blessings, closed the mouths of lions,

- **Healing** The Lord gives us the power to ministry healing by His design.

Acts 4:30. While you stretch out your hand to heal, signs and wonders are performed through the name of your holy servant Jesus.

- **Miracles** The pulling down of the resources and intentions of heaven for God's glory.

Judges 14:6 (Speaking of Samson) 6 The Spirit of the LORD came upon him mightily, and he tore the lion apart as one tears apart a young goat, and he had nothing at all in his hand; but he did not tell his father or mother what he had done.

No one can operate in the ministerial anointing at all times. The Lord releases this when there is a specific assignment given. The Lord described it to me as holding onto a live electrical wire. Your ministerial anointing grows stronger and stronger according to your spiritual maturity. This is related to the level of your relationship with the Lord. Quality time spent in the Word, praying, praying in tongues, praising, and fasting increase your ability to handle increasing levels of this anointing.

The Corporate Anointing- A corporate anointing is present when the anointing spreads to an entire gathering collectively and it multiplies. This is the greatest anointing of all. This is the stuff of group revival. It's when the voices of praise unite into a single voice that is heard and joined with the Angels and greater measures of God's presence are welcomed and experienced.

Praise and worship can bring a corporate anointing when individuals unite together and experience the manifestation of God's anointed presence. The anointing spreads as the blowing of the wind. Sometimes it is sensed as a thick cloud and felt like heaviness, pressing people to the ground. In such an atmosphere, salvations, healings, miracles, deliverances, signs, and wonders have been known to happen. People can often see visions, hear God's voice with greater clarity, and feel themselves being transformed. God's glory is revealed which causes deep levels of repentance and an alignment of God's will and intentions.

I have experienced this level of God's presence and it's indescribable. This is what the Lord had to say about it.

> *It's like everyone in the room has an energy bar with a thermostat that has a temperature and a fan. The temperature is the need or hunger and the fan is the faith level. When you get a lot of people in the same room with the same hunger, the fan goes higher and blows the heat at a greater intensity. A single worship song can raise the anointing level in a room simply by connecting with the hearts of those there. The worship leader can begin the increase with sincere love and worship and then the anointing can spread across the entire congregation. If the leader is not filled with the anointing*

the congregation may feel that disconnect as well. The congregation can also influence the level of anointing that the pastor or worship leader has as well by their passion for Me. Whenever I am multiplied in a room and the entire room is fixing their eyes on Me there will be an increased level of anointing.

The secret to having Me show up in a corporate anointing is not to see that experience. But to sincerely seek Me. I am moved to move by pure hearts that desire more of Me.

Seven Principles that Increase the Anointing:

1. **The Principle of Asking-** We have not because we ask not. We ask not because we desire not. It is our hunger for more and asking God for it that pleases Him and causes Him to give us more.

2. **The Principle of Obedience-** We prove that we can be trusted when we obey the commands in God's word and specific assignments that He gives us. There are specific times and opportunities related to our assignments and the anointing is present during that window of time. Delayed obedience is disobedience.

3. **The Principle of Humility-** The Lord cannot come near pride. We are of no use to the kingdom unless we surrender our sinful nature and remove the various onion layers of pride. Humility and the power of God's grace go hand in hand.

4. **The Principle of Transference-**When you hang around people with great anointing, that anointing rubs off on you. It is transferable from person to person. Spending quality time with Jesus makes His glory and anointing rub off on you.

Elisha hung around Elijah and asked for and received a double portion of his anointing when Elijah was taken up to heaven. (See 2 Kings 2)

5. **The Principle of Worship-** Worshiping God ushers in His presence. Worship attracts the presence of God and when God comes He brings with Him the anointing.

   Psalm 100:4 Enter His gates with a song of thanksgiving
   And His courts with praise.
   Be thankful to Him, bless and praise His name.

6. **The Principle of Retrospection-** When we recall the times we experienced the anointing in the past, we can begin to notice the patterns that influence how often and how much we can experience the anointing again. If He did it before, He can do it again!

7. **The Principle of the Word and Prayer-** Spending time in the Word and in prayer brings illuminated revelation which increases the anointing.

This is what the Lord had to say about increasing the anointing.

Abide in Me. The more faithful you are in seeking My face, reading the Word, and spending time in My presence, the more you will feel the increase of anointing and glory which transforms you into the Christ identity that I created you to become. You are being prepared for your calling by My love and will grow measure by measure in preparation for that calling. This is the season for you to create indelible holy habits of abiding, communion, and worship. These need to become unshakable habits that will be part of your everyday existence. Stay plugged in. Keep desiring more of Me. As you ask for more, I will give you more in increasing stages. Be faithful with the gifts I have given you. They are amazing privileges. Don't take them for granted.

The Spirit of God will not rest on you without your willingness. You must yield to the Holy Spirit to allow Him to come. You need to make Him feel welcome. Watch for when you get in the way. Fear can keep the anointing away and is a form of faithlessness. God made no mistakes when He created and called you. He will use you in your unique way. Don't imitate other people's anointings. God created you with a particular style of anointing for your unique ministry in His kingdom plan. Faith increases the anointing. Little faith yields little results. Great faith yields great results.

How to Intentionally Release the Holy Spirit

1. **Prophetic Words-** The words God spoke in the Bible to the prophets are the truth and life. Jesus is the Word and the Holy Spirit reveals wisdom and understanding about the word in our hearts. When God gives you a word to speak over someone it will always be for their best benefit.

2. **Act of Faith-** God's presence accompanies His actions. Actions are motivated by the compassion and love of God's heart. When you step out in faith to obey God's direct actions it springs forth faith and power. When God directs you to do something, you need to act accordingly and obediently or you will miss a blessing and so will the person for whom you were intended to bless.

3. **Prophetic Actions-** Sometimes what the Lord directs you to do seems illogical. Even if you don't understand why God asking you to do something it's important to obey it. One preacher told the story of how the Lord gave him the assignment to punch a lady in the belly to heal her of stomach cancer. He

obviously double-checked that assignment and obeyed it. Her cancer popped like a balloon and was gone! God knows everything in his ways are wiser than our ways. Imagine how crazy Noah felt obeying that assignment to build an arc in an arid climate for 100 years!

4. **Touch-** The laying of hands is one of the ways that the Lord transfers the anointing from one person to another. I have felt the warmth of God's healing presence in my hands as I have prayed for someone and seen God heal them!

Ways the Holy Spirit is Releasing Without Your Awareness

His Divine Perimeter- When the Holy Spirit overflows from us there is a proximity of the anointing that surrounds us. This is the reason that Peter's shadow healed. It wasn't the shadow itself that healed, it was the divine perimeter of God's anointing. Jesus explained it to me this way:

> Acts 5:14-15 [14] More and more believers in the Lord, crowds of men and women, were constantly being added to their number, [15] to such an extent that they even carried their sick out into the streets and put them on cots and sleeping pads, so that when Peter came by at least his shadow might fall on one of them [with healing power].

This is what Jesus had to say about that.

> *When you are full of the Spirit, the enemy can see and feel Me and they cannot come near My Holiness. The more time you spend in My presence the more lingering of Me there is surrounding you. When people enter this divine radiation zone of My presence they instantly feel Me. Some drop to their knees in repentance when they encounter My Holiness.*

1. **Compassion-** The emotion of God's heart is characterized by love and compassion. Everything God does is motivated by this kingdom emotion. Compassion is different than sympathy. Sympathy gives attention to the person's needs while compassion sets them free. The Lord clarified this further:

   It's all about tapping into the emotions of My heart. I want you to see people's hearts the way I do. Pray "show me their heart" and I will show you what I mean. When you sincerely pray this prayer you will get to the place of compassion. I don't want you to feel sorry for people. That's sympathy. I don't feel sorry for people. I feel love for them. That's what I want you to understand in your heart. It's all about love. Staying tuned to Me is the secret to sensing how I feel about people. That's what you need to understand in your heart to be moved by compassion as I am.

2. **Clothing or other Material Things-** The anointing of the Holy Spirit can be passed on in things like clothing and liquids. An example of this in the Bible is when the woman who had been suffering for twelve years with an illness touched the fringe of Jesus's rope and was healed. The anointing presence on the clothing made the garment holy. This is also another example of the divine perimeter of God's anointing. Jesus was not aware until He felt the healing power leaving His body that this woman had touched his garment. (See Mark 5:21-34)

3. **Worship-** The Holy Spirit inhabits the praises of His people. We can always release His presence and tap into the flow of the Holy Spirit by praising and loving God. The longer you praise God the more likely you will feel His presence. Worship is a form of fixing your eyes on God. When you fix your eyes on Him, He fixes His eyes on you. Where His eyes are fixed, His anointing and glory flow.

How to Abide in the Holy Spirit

The safest place to be is in the center of God's will with the presence of the Holy Spirit protecting you. Stay Holy Spirit-centered. Abiding is a form of dwelling. Living with the Holy Spirit is different than compartmentalizing Him as just a part of your life. It's an immersion lifestyle with a focus on living with the Holy Spirit.

Being with Him is a transformational relationship. You are changed into His likeness when you are around Him. Being with God leads to increased belief and faith in Him. You can't make someone welcome if you don't believe they exist.

> Ephesians 4:30 And do not grieve the Holy Spirit of God [but seek to please Him], by whom you were sealed *and* marked [branded as God's own] for the day of redemption [the final deliverance from the consequences of sin].

To grieve is to cause sorrow and distress. When we don't believe God for who He says He is and what He says He'll do and when we don't invite His presence and surrender to His perfect will we grieve the Spirit.

> 1 Thessalonians 5:18 Do not quench [subdue, or be unre-sponsive to the working and guidance of] the [Holy] Spirit.

To quench is to stop the flow, cut off communion, put out the fire, and extinguish the compassion of God. This reminds me of the importance of staying in the naturally supernatural flow of the Holy Spirit. Knowing that it's important that we stay in the flow is one thing but realizing that it grieves Him when we don't make me even more determined to stay in the spirit of God's presence.

Abiding in God as being conscience of him. We always release the reality of the world we are most aware of. Living with the continual awareness of God must be the supreme goal for anyone who understands the privilege of hosting His spirit. The authority comes with the commission the call or assignment from God. The power comes with the presence of the Holy Spirit. Your service and ministry to the Lord should flow from a relationship with the person of the Holy Spirit who lives in you for your sake and empowers you for the sake of others.

Encountering the Holy Spirit

Choose one of these encounters today, and do the others for home-work. Remember to meet the Lord as a child and allow Him to direct the encounters. Also, beginning each encounter with doing some-thing fun with the Lord is always a great heart-posturing exercise.

1. **A Day with the Holy Spirit-** Ask the Holy Spirit to show you what a day would look like when you lived your daily routine perfectly reflecting God's love and releasing the fragrance of His presence.

2. **Influencers-** Holy Spirit, give me a picture or metaphor to help me understand the things that affect my spirit and show me ways I can allow you to be my greatest influence.

3. **Increase my Sensitivity to your Spirit-** Holy Spirit, how can I have an increase of sensitivity to your Spirit so I may more effectively respond to your flow and obey your voice in my daily walk?

4. **How do I get in your Way?** Holy Spirit, what are ways that my will and spirit get in the way of yours, and How I can release my will more readily, opening the door of your perfect guidance in my life?

100 Billion Times by Hillsong United
https://youtu.be/C2U7ffUM5Ec

Meet the Creator

I cannot think of a better song to represent our Creator than our feature song, *So Will I* (100 Billion Times) by Hillsong United. This song helps us see the power of speaking in agreement with God of creation and connects us with His promises and the meaning of our salvation. It is so beautifully written and reminds us that all nature and creations naturally obey the voice of God except humans. We are the only creature that has been given free will and therefore we much choose to obey the voice of God.

The Creator- Elohim

As mentioned in the previous chapter, the Name of the Creator is *Elohim*. It is a plural name for a singular God. The word trinity cannot be found in the Bible, but Elohim is that word. It shows up as the very first Name of God in Genesis 1:1 and is referenced more than 2,500 times in the original Hebrew bible. Our English translations do not show these unique Hebrew Names but they can be seen in the Names of God (NOG) and the Tree of Life (TLV) translations.

> Genesis 1:1 (NOG) In the beginning **Elohim** created heaven and earth.

The Father is the holder of the will of God. Creation was His idea. Jesus is the Word and the Way, so He was the one speaking in agreement with the will of God. The Holy Spirit is the power of God, so He was the one making creation manifest according to the Word that was spoken.

The entire recounting of the creation is included in Genesis 1 and 2. In this chapter, we will endeavor to understand the Creator by what is revealed about Him through creation. Elohim is a God of incredible order, patterns, and power! In Genesis chapter 1, God created light, the worlds, and life. In Genesis chapter 2 God created mankind and gave us dominion over the earth.

God's Order and Patterns

Answers in Genesis is a wonderful resource for all things related to creation. You can spend months finding answers to your questions about the age of the earth, animals, the Bible, and how science explains the existence of God. This video will give you a short glimpse of the evidence of a Creator as it is compared to a random big bang worldview.

Evidence for Creation
https://answersingenesis.org/evidence-for-creation/

The Fingerprint of God

God's order is evident in creation, but a scientist in the 11th century was able to mathematically identify a pattern in nature that is simply mind-boggling. This video will explain it much better than I could. Like me, after watching this, I hope you will begin to see these patterns more in everyday life.

Fibonacci Sequence/The Fingerprint of God
https://youtu.be/fX8gy9EWZ_Y

Frequency of God's Love- God's Omnibenevolence

God is love. He spoke the world into existence and sustains it with His power. At the most basic level, everything has a frequency. When God created the universe, the newly created atoms were spinning harmoniously according to the vibration of His created order. They were programmed to respond to the voice of God. God is not only the Creator but the sustainer of all of His creation.

Colossians 1:16-17 **16** For [a]by Him all things were created in heaven and on earth, [things] visible and invisible, whether thrones or dominions or rulers or authorities; all things were created *and* exist through Him [that is, by His activity] and for Him. [17] And He Himself existed *and* is before all things, and in Him all things hold together. [His is the controlling, cohesive force of the universe.]

But why did God create everything? We learn His motivation in Acts.

Acts 17:26-28 [26] And He made from one *man* every nation of mankind to live on the face of the earth, having determined their appointed times and the boundaries of their lands *and* territories. [27] This was so that they would seek God, if perhaps they might grasp for Him and find Him, though He is not far from each one of us. [28] For in Him we live and move and exist [that is, in Him we actually have our being], as even some of [a]your own poets have said, 'For we also are His children.'

Elohim made it all so He could have a relationship with you and me. Everything God does is motivated by love not because He feels love, but because He IS love. His heart longing as revealed in this verse is for us to want to love Him back. God loves us unconditionally. His perfect love is His Omnibenevolence. Omni means perfect, complete, and full.

Romans 8:38-39 [38] For I am convinced [and continue to be convinced—beyond any doubt] that neither death, nor life, nor angels, nor principalities, nor things present *and* threatening, nor things to come, nor powers, [39] nor height, nor depth, nor any other created thing, will be able to separate us from the [unlimited] love of God, which is in Christ Jesus our Lord.

God's love is heaven's tuning fork of God's perfect vibration of love. When Adam and Eve sinned for the first time, it broke our natural ability to connect with God's love. But, Jesus' finished work on the cross restored our ability to be able to tap into that love vibration by using the eyes and ears of our hearts to once again connect with His heart.

Other Creatures vs Mankind

Man is the only creature that has been given free will. Sin is a transgression of God's laws. We know that sin did not exist at the time of creation because God proclaimed everything as good. And He proclaimed man as very good.

All other creatures were created to perfectly obey God's laws and exist in their uniquely created habitats according to their natural instincts. When Adam and Eve sinned, they broke God's laws and therefore placed a curse on the entire world. Sin entered the world. Animals do not sin because they were not the ones that broke the laws and were not created with a moral compass. But they are subjected to the consequences of man's decisions and live in a fallen world as we do.[10]

Animals follow God's design and naturally obey the rules of God. We call these animal instincts. Some animal species show emotions such as loyalty and faithfulness exemplified by penguins who mate for life. Birds and other species have revealed a self-protective pre-knowledge of natural disasters.

In a previous book, I shared a journal that the Lord gave me about how some animals are anointed for ministry as evidenced by their unconditional love and ability to comfort people. The Lord shared with me that those animals go to heaven when they die.

People are the only creatures that do not naturally obey God. We must choose to obey God. Mankind was given dominion over all created things.

---

[10] https://www.gotquestions.org/do-animals-sin.html

Genesis 1:26-27 (NOG) [26] Then **Elohim** said, "Let us make humans in our image, in our likeness. Let them rule the fish in the sea, the birds in the sky, the domestic animals all over the earth, and all the animals that crawl on the earth."

[27] So Elohim created humans in his image.
In the image of Elohim He created them.
He created them male and female.

Man can mess up the ecosystems of animals with our free will decisions that disrupt that natural order of things. Poachers that kill off a single species can mess up the food supply to the microscopic bacterial level and devastate an untold number of creatures and even affect people.

Environmentalists have identified certain "keystone species" which if were to be eliminated could end life as we know it. Their roles within the ecosystem are so critical that their elimination would collapse the entire ecosystem. African termites, bumble bees, and Grizzly bears are three examples of keystone species.

To rule the earth and take care of the Lord's creation is an important responsibility. Unfortunately, we have not done a great job of this and the evidence of our fallen nature is proof of that.

Deuteronomy 30:19-20 [19] I call heaven and earth as witnesses against you today, that I have set before you life and death, the blessing and the curse; therefore, you shall choose life in order that you may live, you and your descendants, [20] by loving the LORD your God, by obeying His voice, and by holding closely to Him; for He is your life [your good life, your abundant life, your fulfillment] and the length of your days, that you may live in the land which the LORD promised (swore) to give to your fathers, to Abraham, Isaac, and Jacob."

Light

The first thing that Elohim decided to create was light. God is light.

> 1 John 1:5 ⁵This is the message [of God's promised revelation] which we have heard from Him and now announce to you, that God is Light [He is holy, His message is truthful, He is perfect in righteousness], and in Him there is no darkness at all [no sin, no wickedness, no imperfection].

God created natural light to reflect His supernatural light. Light casts out all darkness, both literally and spiritually. There were many biblical examples of people encountering God's supernatural light. When Moses was on the mountain for example as God was writing the 10 Commandments with His finger, Moses returned down the mountain and his face reflected God's light. (See Exodus 34:29-34).

Saul was blinded by the light of Jesus when he encountered Him on the road to Damascus. (See Acts 9). The angels that appeared to the shepherds on the night of Jesus' birth lit up the sky with their light. (See Luke 2). All of these stories have one thing in common, the Presence of God. When you encounter God in His glory, you encounter the light of God.

God's Omniscience

God is the source of all knowledge and wisdom. We learn in Matthew 10:30 that the very hairs on your head are numbered. And in Psalms 147:4-5 we learn that the Lord knows the number of all of our stars of the universe and calls them all by name. Scientists estimate that there are between 150 and 200 billion stars in the Milky Way galaxy of which our sun is but one.

In Job 38, the Lord goes on for quite a few verses about all the things He created to give Job and us a greater understanding of His omniscience and power. His wisdom extends far beyond our earthly capabilities and worldly dimension.

We should never take pride in what we know about science as though science itself is greater than the Creator of the truth of scientific discoveries. Just because you understand how something can be, doesn't mean you could have created it.

The Quantum Physics Realities - God's Omnipresence

Scientists have learned that the laws of the physical world including such things as relativity and gravity are different than those of the quantum or microscopic world.

The physical world is characterized as local, which means that everything you can see can be charted and found. It has a defined location. The quantum as well as the spiritual realm are identified as non-local. That means that they are nonphysical dimensions and have no geographical location.

The properties of non-locality are that there is constant movement spinning and vibrating. Particles have a ghost-link between each other. This is a connection that causes them to spin or move in sync. Scientists call this connection quantum entanglement.

Quantum entanglement is like a prophetic parable. Because we are citizens of heaven as well as the earth. We have Christ in us, and Christ has us in Him. We are tethered to Him, inseparable from the Lord once we have received the gift of salvation. What Christ does affects you. What you do affects Him. Because of your dual citizenship, you can be bi-locational. You can live naturally supernaturally, sensing

Him in your spirit while living and allowing God's glory to influence the world around you in the natural world.

> Ephesians 2:6 ⁶ And He raised us up together with Him [when we believed], and seated us with Him in the heavenly *places*, [because we are] in Christ Jesus,

Note the present tense in that verse. The moment that you believed, you were seated with Jesus in heavenly places. It says because you are in Christ Jesus. So we learn here that you don't need to die and go to heaven to be seated with Jesus in heavenly places. Your spirit is already there and here with you now. When you have encounters with the Lord in the spirit, you are engaging with heaven while still on earth. Perhaps this gives you a new level of insight into what Jesus meant when he said in Matthew chapter 5 "Your kingdom come, Your will be done on earth as it is in heaven."

The Observer Effect

Perhaps the most interesting thing I learned about quantum physics while researching for this chapter was related to the observer effect. Scientists have unanimously agreed that when we look at something we change it. At the quantum level, particles behave non-locally, simply floating around until they are observed, and then they collapse into matter. The act of observing is the only factor that creates this change. Scientists call this behavior the wave function collapse and essentially it means that something from an invisible realm becomes visible when looked at.

Let's take the above reality to the next level of understanding. The physical universe as we know it and as we experience it every single day is collapsed into a material state because it's being observed.

How is it then that we are pretty certain that isolated areas of the world where no people are watching them still exist in physical form? Because the omnipresent God is looking at it! His eyes are on everything in this and all other worlds from the infinitesimally small to the magnanimously large at all times.

When you become saved and received Jesus in your heart, and were baptized in the Holy Spirit, you received the full capability to observe Jesus in the spiritual realm. Every possibility is available to you in Christ when we understand your abilities to be in this earthly realm and the spiritual realm simultaneously. All healing, provision, direction, and wisdom are at your fingertips when you keep your eyes fixed on Jesus.

> 2 Corinthians 3:18 [18] And we all, with unveiled face, *continually* seeing as in a mirror the glory of the Lord, are *progressively* being transformed into His image from [one degree of] glory to [even more] glory, which comes from the Lord, [who is] the Spirit.

The more you fix your eyes on Jesus, the more you are transformed into His image. Observing Him changes you. It also causes Him to observe you which changes Him. This even more focused gazing on God's part moves Hin to move on your behalf in this exchange.

Words and Speaking- God's Omnipotence

The Lord creates by speaking. His Word is His will. When God speaks He energizes creative power. The word for energy in the Bible is *energeo* which means I work, I accomplish, to display, properly, energize, working *in* a situation which brings it from one stage (point) to the next. We have already learned, that the world collapsed into material matter because the Lord looked at it. All sound creates vibration. There is hearing and seeing involved in creation.

100

Hebrews 1:3a [3] The Son is the radiance *and* only expression of the glory of [our awesome] God [reflecting God's [a] Shekinah glory, the Light-being, the brilliant light of the divine], and the exact representation *and* perfect imprint of His [Father's] essence, and upholding *and* maintaining *and* propelling all things [the entire physical and spiritual universe] by His powerful word [carrying the universe along to its predetermined goal].

Here we learn that God's word maintains the creation for as long as needed for His plans to be completed. As He never stops looking, He never stops speaking. The vibration of God's speaking voice maintains the entire physical and spiritual worlds. I remember once the Lord telling me that He held His breath, all creation would cease to exist. Now I am convinced, that if He blinked all creation would cease to exist as well!

You were spoken into being God's voice. You were created in God's image so you create with your words too. Here is a quick list of truths related to words with some scripture references.

- Words are powerful-Proverbs 18:21 "Death and life are in the power of the tongue, and those who love it will eat its fruit."

- Build others up with our words- Proverbs 18:4- the person's words can be life-giving water: words of true wisdom are as refreshing as a bubbling brook.

- Words reveal the condition of your heart- Proverbs 25:18 telling lies about others is as harmful as hitting them with an ax, or wounding them with the sword, or shooting them with the sharp arrow.

- Guard your mouth- Proverbs 21:23 whosoever keeps his mouth and his tongue keeps himself out of trouble.

- Speak God's Word- Matthew 4:4 but Jesus answered, "it is written, Man shall not live by bread alone, but by every word that comes out of the mouth of God.

- You will have to give an account for your words- Matthew 12:36 but I tell you that every careless word that people speak, they shall give an account for it in the day of judgment.

- Your words reveal a changed heart- Colossians 4:6 let your speech always be gracious, seasoned with salt, so that you may know how you ought to answer each person.

Speak Life!

String Theory

String theory is one of the controversial quantum theories which an increasing number of scientists are embracing as a possibility. It is an attempt to understand the connection between the physical and quantum worlds. The theory hypothesizes the existence of tiny strings or loops of vibrating energy that act as the building blocks of all aspects of the world.

The theory has been mathematically developed and suggests hidden dimensions curled up or folded within our three-dimensional world. Tiny loops of vibrating energy are constantly moving as extra-dimensional fields of energy. They are like-minded strings of vibrating energy. The math suggests that these strings are 100 billion times smaller than a proton. So it is unlikely that the naked eye will ever be able to create technology that would allow us to see that.

Christian expert on string theory, Brian Green wrote a book called *The Elegant Universe.* In it, he shared that no two strings vibrate at the same frequency. This reinforces the complexity and unique nature of God's creation. God reveals His artistic stamp on all that He creates. For those who understand the patterns seen in the mathematics of string theory, there is an artistic beauty about it. This is why Brian Greene entitled his book the elegant universe suggesting that if our ears could hear the sounds of these various vibrations it would sound like an elegant symphony.

Phil Mason, in his book *Quantum Glory,* wrote; "The quantum world has been intentionally designed to obey the voice of God. When God speaks His creative word the entire quantum field can be rearranged, collapsed, or reconstructed at His command. There is a remarkable convergence between these two theological concepts in the Bible and the emergence of the string theory. To my mind biblical theology powerfully supports string theory, not just because of the convergence of notions of extra dimensionality or the elegance in design but because of the energizing relationship between the Spirit of God and the strings that perhaps constitute nature at its very smallest scale. String theorists suggest that these strings vibrated different frequencies to create a sub-atomic Symphony of music."

I asked the Lord to show me something to help me if string theory was real, and if so, how I can understand it. I was immediately reminded of the *Horton Hears a Who* film clip that the Lord had me share in *Encountering the DIRECTION of God, Book 3* of this series. It was about how an entire civilization could exist on a single speck size of dust in the physical realm but the large world could not see or comprehend it.

Then God showed me a tiny white wiggling loop. Then He zoomed out the vision to a dozen or so spinning, vibrating, and wiggling white loops and strings. Then zoomed out till there were likely thousands of them looking now more like a wavelike movement together. Finally, He zoomed it out millions were inside a single proton. It was like the entire Who world on the speck! Jesus explained;

> *Like all of nature, these strings obey My Voice. My voice is what creates the vibrations for them to keep on moving. They do what I say with 100% obedience.*
>
> *When you fix your eyes on Me and speak and do what I say, they obey your voice because you are echoing My voice. They form connections and begin to play the symphony at OUR command.*

> God is always speaking!

My Flying Carpet Encounter

In the Encountering the DIRECTION of God Conclusion chapter, I shared my first encounter with the Lord where He showed me the strings connecting people in the body of Christ in their destiny caves. Below is a flying carpet adventure the Lord gave me as a follow-up to that one.

As my five-year-old childlike self with my lion stuffed animal in hand, I burst through the back patio door of my special place. I saw my fish tank, my cat Tazzie on the patio, and the other animals playing in the yard. Maureen was there and she took me by my hand and transported me to my destiny cave. Jesus was sitting on the stone balcony, dangling His legs over the colorful River of Living Water below.

Jesus invited me to sit with Him there when the flying carpet flew up to us. Just like the one in the Aladdin movie, it seemed to say hello to me with its corner tassel. This made me smile. Jesus and I jumped on top of the flying carpet and we were flying over the river past other destiny caves going higher and higher. There were millions of destiny caves with their rock balconies peppered throughout this entire place. Then like in my previous vision, Jesus showed me the white strings of light connecting all of these caves. The strings were connecting the servants of God as they ministered according to their destinies. There were so many string connections it reminded me of a giant spirograph. Then from the strings of light, I saw the raindrops watering the entire canyon creating a beautiful rainbow of color everywhere I could see. Living water was refreshing and growing everything it touched. Then Jesus said to me:

> *I am the Sovereign Lord! My purposes will be done through these servants and their connections. This is the season of the great harvest. My plan will be done through all of the servants. Their connections are like the linking of puzzle pieces into one beautiful tapestry of my Kingdom plan.*

The Spirit vs Earthly Realms- God's Omnipotence

Elohim created both the physical and the spiritual realms, the visible and invisible worlds.

> Colossians 1:16 **16** For [a]by Him all things were created in heaven and on earth, [things] visible and invisible, whether thrones or dominions or rulers or authorities; all things were created *and* exist through Him [that is, by His activity] and for Him.

We have already learned that speaking and observing can manifest the invisible will of God into the physical material world. Miracles defy natural physics but can be understood in quantum physics.

> Hebrews 11:3 **3** By faith [that is, with an inherent trust and enduring confidence in the power, wisdom and goodness of

God] we understand that the worlds (universe, ages) were framed *and* created [formed, put in order, and equipped for their intended purpose] by the word of God, so that what is seen was not made out of things which are visible.

Many verses topically address the veil in the Bible. The veil represents the barrier between you and God. It can be a mental barrier or a physical one as was in the Tabernacle. When you fix your eyes on Jesus, He allows you to see things from His perspective He removes the veil. There is no barrier when you can see what He sees, say what He says, feel what He feels, and think His thoughts.

> 2 Corinthians 3:15-18 (MSG) [15] Only Christ can get rid of the veil so they can see for themselves that there's nothing there.
>
> [16-18] Whenever, though, they turn to face God as Moses did, God removes the veil and there they are—Face-to-face! They suddenly recognize that God is a living, personal presence, not a piece of chiseled stone. And when God is personally present, a living Spirit, that old, constricting legislation is recognized as obsolete. We're free of it! All of us! Nothing between us and God, our faces shining with the brightness of his face. And so we are transfigured much like the Messiah, our lives gradually becoming brighter and more beautiful as God enters our lives and we become like him.

When the veil is removed, there is an opening to connect the spiritual realm to the physical realm. So whenever you fix your eyes on Jesus and tune to Him by way of the Holy Spirit, you are stepping through from the physical dimension into the spiritual one. Understanding that you have the authority is critical to being able to exercise the power that comes with that authority.

When Jesus died, the veil in the temple was ripped from top to bottom. This signified that the barrier that separated you from intimacy with God was removed. You now have the opportunity for direct access to the very heart of God available to you.

Speaking of the quantum world, Phil Mason explains the veil in this way; "As we explore this dimension of non-local quantum reality in greater depth, I will propose that this invisible layer of quantum reality acts as some kind of interface between the presence and the power of God (who exists in the spiritual realm) and the world of matter. The non-local quantum world appears to be a kind of invisible, intermediate "buffer zone" between spirit and matter. It appears that the nonlocal quantum realm has been strategically crafted by God to be directly responsive to the influence of the activity of the spirit of God so these nonlocal quantum realities are capable of "materializing" into a localized spatial formation. Quantum realities are the building blocks of all matter."[11]

There are many examples in the Bible of materialism and de-materialism miracles. All of these miracles defy the physical rules of our world. Jesus turned water into wine or multiplied the loaves and the fish. Elijah was taken up to heaven by chariots of fire. Jesus appeared before the Disciples post-resurrection from nowhere. Philip was instantly transported 13 miles away as the Ethiopian man he was baptizing rose out of the water. (See Acts 8:39) These are just some of the Biblical examples of how God shows us what can be done when we live a life without the limitations of a veil. Supernatural things happen when you know God's abilities and by extension, your capabilities, and authority as His child.

Understanding Glory

God's Glory is His transformational presence. It essentially shows you His holy righteousness. When you are faced with what is right, you

---

[11] Mason, Phil. Quantum Glory: The Science of Heaven Invading Earth (pp. 87). XP Publishing. Kindle Edition.

immediately are shown what is wrong. God's fire is a purifying light. It is not a destructive fire but a cleansing one. Encountering God's glory purifies and burns off things that hinder. It helps to make you see yourself clearly and molds you into God's likeness, nature, and character.

When Ezekiel faced the God of glory in the throne room he fell on his face for seven days. When Daniel saw God he lost all strength and passed out into a deep sleep. When Peter saw Jesus do something miraculous, he fell at his feet and said depart from me Lord, for I am a sinner. Facing the glory of God has you see yourself rightly and causes immediate humility in repentance.

The Glory of God is the beauty of His Spirit. It reveals His nature and His character. We learned about the Creator through His creation. He reveals His love through His creation. God created us for His Glory (See Isaiah 43:7) This means that His will is for us to align with Him. To become reflections of His glory to the world. He created us to reflect His love and light in a dark world. When we release the beauty of God's loving character and nature, we reveal His glory.

To be received into Glory is an expression that means to go to heaven, where God's Glory abounds.

Combining Seeing and Hearing in Obedience

The Father conceived of the idea of creation. The Son spoke it, and the Holy Spirit manifested it. Elohim saw that it was good. Now the Trinity keeps looking and speaking and creation obeys His voice maintaining it. All creation is sustained by God looking and speaking. I know that in every one of these Experience Jesus books I bring up the importance of cooperating and living in sync with God.

John 5:30 [30] "I can do nothing on my own initiative *or* authority. Just as I hear, I judge; and My judgment is just (fair, righteous, unbiased), because I do not seek My own will, but only the will of Him who sent Me.

Jesus always obeys the will of the Father.

John 8:28 [28] So Jesus said, "When you lift up the Son of Man [on the cross], you will know then [without any doubt] that I am *He*, and that I do nothing on My own authority, but I say these things just as My Father taught Me.

You can grow into increasing proficiency at living bi-dimensionally so that you can naturally do and say what you see and hear Jesus doing. This is what we call living out of your Christ-Identity naturally supernaturally. It is possible to live this way. You are a dual citizen of heaven and earth. When you understand the authority you have to see and hear Jesus in the spirit and obey His voice, miracles can be a daily normal occurrence.

Jesus commanded His disciples to follow His example and told them that if they did, they would see even greater things.

John 5:19-20 (MSG) [19-20] So Jesus explained himself at length. "I'm telling you this straight. The Son can't independently do a thing, only what he sees the Father doing. What the Father does, the Son does. The Father loves the Son and includes him in everything he is doing.

[20-23] "But you haven't seen the half of it yet, for in the same way that the Father raises the dead and creates life, so does the Son. The Son gives life to anyone he chooses. Neither he nor the Father shuts anyone out. The Father handed all authority to judge over to the Son so that the Son will be honored equally with the Father. Anyone who dishonors the Son, dishonors the Father, for it was the Father's decision to put the Son in the place of honor.

Jesus explained the essential nature of the connection He wanted us to have with Him in John 15.

John 15:5 [5] [a]I am the Vine; you are the branches. The one who remains in Me and I in him bears much fruit, for [otherwise] apart from Me [that is, cut off from vital union with Me] you can do nothing.

Just as Jesus could do nothing apart from the Father, we can do nothing apart from Jesus. I have lost count of all of the miracles I have seen God do because I understand this principle and pray according to it. And so can you! When God shows you something by way of the Holy Spirit, show you agree by speaking the words and obeying the actions as you see the Lord directing you.

Lord, what more do you have to say about you as the Creator and us as creators in You?

My creation reveals My glory, love, and power. Oddly, the more that scientists discover about my worlds, the more they doubt My existence. Even though things are so complex and orderly, the increasing knowledge of people causes arrogance and they still deny Me.

In simpler days, people respected the wonder of My creation. They did not doubt the existence of a Creator. It was obvious that no man could create from nothing the stars, the sun, the moon, and all of the planets or the worlds of the seas, land, and sky.

Adam and Eve ate from the Tree of Knowledge of Good and Evil. This is the tree of self-knowledge and understanding. This kind of knowledge leaves Me out. There is no power when you leave Me out.

You need to understand the power you have as a dual citizen of heaven and earth. Those saved and chosen ones who have never activated the Holy Spirit in their hearts will begin to

110

sense Me more in the season of later days. Experience is a mighty teacher and no one can deny a person's life experience with Me. This is why testimonials are so important and powerful. Your stories of how I was made real to you carry the power of creation to heal and transform.

I am bigger than anyone can ever understand. I am constantly looking at everything from the infinitesimally micro to the magnanimously macro. Nothing escapes My eye. I even see into the hearts of My people. And so can you when you stay tuned to Me as you share in My divine nature.

I exist inside and outside of the physical realm. So can you. Ask me to show you how to live simultaneously in both realities. Keep your eyes fixed on Me. This is the door, the gateway that gains you access the see, think, feel, and most importantly know My will. When you live out of this perspective you will always know what to say and what to do. You will know how to pull heaven down to earth one assignment at a time.

Encountering the Creator

Remember to meet the Lord as a child and allow Him to direct the encounters. Also, beginning each encounter with doing something fun with the Lord is always a great heart-posturing exercise.

1. **Jump into the Bible - Show me Creation!** Elohim, take me on an adventure and show me glimpses of when you created the universe and everything in it. Explain to me what you were doing and why you did it. Prepare for this encounter by first meditating on Genesis Chapters 1 and 2.

2. **Show me Your Glory-** Creator God, show me how to increase my awareness of you. Show me your Glory in earthly and heavenly realms.

3. **See in the Spirit-** Lord, strengthen the eyes of my heart. Give me specific tips and tools that will help me to see in the Spirit realm what you need me to see.

4. **Hear You in the Spirit-** Lord increase my sensitivity to Your Voice. Give me specific tips and tools that will help me to hear You more easily and not doubt your voice.

El Shaddai by Amy Grant
https://youtu.be/clt8BoHb0JE

Meet God Almighty

The first incidence of the introduction of the Name God Almighty is found in Genesis 17:1

Genesis 17:1 [*Abraham and the Covenant of Circumcision*] When Abram was ninety-nine years old, the LORD appeared to him and said, "I am **God Almighty**; Walk [habitually] before Me [with integrity, knowing that you are always in My presence], and be blameless *and* complete [in obedience to Me].

The Hebrew name for God Almighty is *El Shaddai*. It is a compound name, El refers to God's "is-ness". Shaddai refers to His "does-ness."

The "is-ness" of God is anything that He IS. It is His full identity. El, Jehovah, Yahweh, and I AM are all names that address God's Is-ness. He is love, for example. Love is not what He feels, it is who He is. We learned about this in the first book of this Experience Jesus series entitled *Encountering the LOVE of God.*

God IS self-existent. This means He is not a created being but always was, is, and will always be. Because God was things before He created the world and everyone in it, we can have no impact on those aspects of Him.

Shaddai emphasizes His "does-ness, that is what He does. This word means omnipotent ruler of all. When this name is used it's emphasizing God's power to fulfill His promises. Almighty means that all strength and power are sourced from God. Omnipotence is part of the Is-ness of God. However, this is the characteristic that Abraham was observing when he referred to God as Almighty in Genesis 17:1.

There are 58 verses in the Names of God translation (NOG) That reference The name El Shaddai. I sorted them by the categories; who He Is, what He does, and what He wants from you. Each subword can have hundreds of more verses. For example, Holy/Holiness has 611 verses in the AMP version.

Who He IS

God Introduced Himself to Abraham by this Name in Genesis 17 as a way to reveal the promise of his uncountable descendants. As impossible as it was to imagine a man at the age of 99 fathering a child, it would require a tremendous amount of power to accomplish such a thing through a wife that was also in her 90s.

There are four major emphases of the identity of God Almighty; His Omnipotence, Righteousness and Sovereignty, and Holiness.

- **Omnipotence** – *Shaddai*

  Rev 11:15-17 (AMP [15] Then the seventh angel sounded His trumpet]; and there were loud voices in heaven, saying,

  "The kingdom (dominion, rule) of the world has become *the kingdom* of our Lord and of His Christ; and He will reign forever and ever." [16] And the twenty-four elders, who sit on their thrones before God, fell face downward and worshiped God, [17] saying,

"To You we give thanks, O Lord God Almighty [the Omnipotent, the Ruler of all], Who are and Who were, because You have taken Your great power *and* the sovereignty [which is rightly Yours] and have [now] begun to reign.

- **Righteous**- *tsaddiq* means blameless, just, fair, innocent, who was, is, and always will be.

Ezra 9:19 O LORD God of Israel, You are [uncompromisingly] just (righteous), for we have been left as survivors, as it is this day. Behold, we are before You in our guilt, for no one can stand before You because of this."

- **Sovereign**- *despotés* which means exercising complete jurisdiction and power. Absolute power because of absolute authority.

Acts 4:23-24 [23] After Peter and John were released, they returned to their own [people] and reported everything that the chief priests and elders had said to them. [24] And when they heard it, they raised their voices together to God and said, "O Sovereign Lord [having complete power and authority], it is You who MADE THE HEAVEN AND THE EARTH AND THE SEA, AND EVERYTHING THAT IS IN THEM,

- **Holy**- *hagios* means set apart, sacred, the likeness and nature of God, different than the world, distinguishable as God-like.

Revelation 4:8 [8] And the four living creatures, each one of them having six wings, are full of eyes all over and within [underneath their wings]; and day and night they never stop saying,

"HOLY, HOLY, HOLY [is the] LORD GOD, THE ALMIGHTY [the Omnipotent, the Ruler of all], WHO WAS AND WHO IS AND WHO IS TO COME [the unchanging, eternal God]."

What He DOES

- **Blesses/Favors-** It was interesting to me how many of the verses about Almighty God were about His blessing and favor. I believe this reinforces God's heart motivation of love behind everything He does. He created us to be fruitful. In the Old Testament context, this looked like having children. In the New Testament context, it is about releasing His power for Kingdom impact.

  Gen 28:3 May [a]God Almighty bless you and make you fruitful and multiply you, so that you may become a [great] company of peoples.

- **Disciplines-** God lovingly disciplines His children for building character and helping us to align ourselves to His likeness and purposes.

  Job 5:17 Behold, how happy *and* fortunate is the man whom God reproves, So do not despise *or* reject the discipline of the Almighty [subjecting you to trial and suffering].

- **Exercises Justice-** The Almighty God is exalted in power and will not disregard justice. He responds to the cries of His righteous people.

  Luke 18:7 And will not [our just] God defend *and* avenge His elect [His chosen ones] who cry out to Him day and night? Will He delay [in providing justice] on their behalf?

- **Protects/ Fights for Us-** The big lesson for us here is to allow the Lord to do the fighting for us. Too often we leave Him behind and try to fight battles that are His to fight on our behalf. But when we dwell in the shelter of His presence, we know when to be still and allow Him to do the fighting for us and with us. No enemy can withstand His power!

Psalm 91:1- He who [a]dwells in the shelter of the Most High Will remain secure *and* rest in the shadow of the Almighty [whose power no enemy can withstand].

- **Gives Wisdom-** The Holy Spirit's presence in your heart includes the mind of Christ. You can tap into the very wisdom of God in your heart through the experiences you can have with God in these encounters.

Job 32:8 "But there is [a vital force and] a spirit [of intelligence] in man, And the breath of the Almighty gives them understanding.

- **Influences Behaviors and Emotions** – Emotions are what cause people to act. Jesus was motivated by compassion. When you align your heart with the Lord, you can know who He wants you to become and what He wants you to do. This alignment leads to fruitfulness. First, you are transformed into the person He sees you as already, your Christ-Identity. Then you begin to take the actions needed to fulfill your kingdom's purpose.

Gen 35:11 [11] And God said to him, "I am [a]God Almighty. Be fruitful and multiply; A nation and a company of nations shall come from you, And kings shall be born of your [b]loins.

Three Things He Desires from You

There were three major categories of things that God desires from you to receive power from God Almighty; for you to have a relationship with Him, to be like Him, and to exercise your authority as His Child.

For You to have a Relationship with Him

- **Diligently seek His face-** To seek God's face and not His hand is to desire Him over what you want from Him. To want who

He is and not what He can do for you. Oddly, wanting Him more than wanting what He can do for you motivates His heart to do more for you than you could have ever asked for. His heart is for you to want the Healer more than the healing, to want the Blesser more than the blessing.

Job 8:5-6 [5] "If you would [diligently] seek God And implore the compassion *and* favor of the Almighty, [6] Then, if you are pure and upright, Surely now He will awaken for you And restore your righteous place.

- **To hear His voice and seek His vision-** We learned in the introduction to this book that the Lord created everything and everyone so He could have intimacy with people. He gave each of us the eyes and ears of our hearts to enable us to connect with Him.

Num 24:4 The oracle of one who hears the words of God, Who sees the vision of the Almighty, falling down, but having his eyes open *and* uncovered,

- **To walk in His presence -** Jesus never did anything on His own, but only what He saw and heard the Father doing. This is God's mandate for us. We cannot have a relationship with Him or obey His voice if we close our eyes and ears to Him. To walk habitually means that it is your everyday normal posture. It means a lifestyle of abiding.

Gen 17:1 When Abram was ninety-nine years old, the [a] Lord appeared to him and said, "I AM [b]God Almighty; Walk [habitually] before Me [with integrity, knowing that you are always in My presence], and be blameless and complete [in obedience to Me].

- **To make Him our greatest treasure and lift our faces to Him-** To treasure something means that it is extremely valuable to you. It is a high priority for you. What you treasure is easy to identify. It is what you spend your time, talents, and your focus on. God wants to be your greatest treasure. You will fix your eyes on things you treasure. When you fix your eyes on Him as part of your lifestyle, you are proving that He is your greatest treasure.

Job 22:25-26 [25] And make the Almighty your gold and your precious silver, [26] Then you will have delight in the Almighty, And you will lift up your face to God.

To Be Like Him

- **To be holy-** Holiness is being set apart. To live out the holiness that God has called us to, we must surrender all that is "self" as a sacred living sacrifice. To live in holiness is to experience the delights of direct communion with God and it is a genuine expression of worship. Obedience to God's call to holiness is a sweet-smelling aroma to God.

See all of 1 Thessalonians 4 for more on holiness.

1Thessalonians 4:3,7 [3] For this is the will of God, that you be sanctified [separated and set apart from sin]:... [7] For God has not called us to impurity, but to holiness [to be dedicated, and set apart by behavior that pleases Him, whether in public or in private].

- **To be righteous-** When you stop trying to be righteous and simply trust the Holy Spirit to change your heart, He will make you righteous.

See all of Romans 12.

Romans 12:2 And do not be conformed to this world [any longer with its superficial values and customs], but be [c]

121

transformed *and* progressively changed [as you mature spiritually] by the renewing of your mind [focusing on godly values and ethical attitudes], so that you may prove [for yourselves] what the will of God is, that which is good and acceptable and perfect [in His plan and purpose for you].

• **To be transformed into His Likeness with His nature and character-** God is perfectly righteous and holy. We could never be those things apart from Him. But thank God that He has equipped us with this ability as we grow and mature in Christ. It is still a choice we must make to access and release God's nature and character.

Romans 8:29-30 [29] For those whom He foreknew [and loved and chose beforehand], He also predestined to be conformed to the image of His Son [and ultimately share in His complete sanctification], so that He would be the firstborn [the most beloved and honored] among many believers. [30] And those whom He predestined, He also called; and those whom He called, He also justified [declared free of the guilt of sin]; and those whom He justified, He also glorified [raising them to a heavenly dignity].

To exercise our Authority as Children of God

• **Be fruitful and multiply-** In the Old Testament days, this was literally about having children and growing families. But in the New Testament context, fruitfulness is about your Kingdom impact. It is about multiplying the number of believers and disciplining the nations.

Gen 35:11 [11] And God said to him,
"I am [a]God Almighty.
Be fruitful and multiply;

A nation and a company of nations shall come from you,
And kings shall be born of your [b]loins.

- **To obey his voice and commands-** Obedience is a staple of Christian maturity. God's ways are always better than ours and His will leads to blessings and favor. Jesus perfectly fulfilled the law, so obeying Him is obeying God's commandments.

Ecclesiastes 12:13 When all has been heard, the end of the matter is: fear God [worship Him with awe-filled reverence, knowing that He is almighty God] and keep His commandments, for this applies to every person.

- **To release His compassion and favor-**

Job 8:5-6 ⁵"If you would [diligently] seek God
And implore the compassion *and* favor of the Almighty,
⁶ Then, if you are pure and upright,
Surely now He will awaken for you
And restore your righteous place.

- **Wield the Sword of the Spirit-** The Word of God is the Sword of the Spirit, and it is the only weapon mentioned in the Armor of God The other aspects of the Armor are all used for protection. Notice that there is no protective gear for the back. This is because when you turn your back on God, you lose your protection. (See Ephesians 6:10-23.)

Ephesians 6:13-17 ¹³ Therefore, put on the complete armor of God, so that you will be able to [successfully] resist *and* stand your ground in the evil day [of danger], and having done everything [that the crisis demands], to stand firm [in your place, fully prepared, immovable, victorious]. ¹⁴ So stand firm *and* hold your ground, HAVING [b]TIGHTENED THE WIDE BAND OF TRUTH (personal integrity, moral courage) AROUND YOUR WAIST and HAVING PUT ON THE

BREASTPLATE OF RIGHTEOUSNESS (an upright heart), [15] and having [c]strapped on YOUR FEET THE GOSPEL OF PEACE IN PREPARATION [to face the enemy with firm-footed stability and the readiness produced by the good news]. [16] Above all, lift up the [protective] [d]shield of faith with which you can extinguish all the flaming arrows of the evil *one*. [17] And take THE HELMET OF SALVATION, and the sword of the Spirit, which is the Word of God.

The Kingdom of Heaven

The Kingdom of Heaven is a Spiritual realm. I asked the Lord to help me understand it and initially, He gave me the words *around, among, and inside*. I asked Him to clarify:

> *The Kingdom of heaven is around, among, and inside of you. It is all centered around My will. You learned when you studied the Creator, that there is a veil separating the spiritual and physical worlds. The spiritual realm is around you with angels helping, protecting, and intervening on your behalf. Demons are also around you menacing as you give them authority to do so. An entire world of spiritual activity surrounds people without their awareness. In this sense, the Kingdom is around you.*
>
> *There is also the activity of the Headquarters of Heaven. This is like the command central for all spiritual activity.*
>
> *Because the Holy Spirit dwells in the hearts of believers, the fullness of Godhead is inside of you. So, the Kingdom is inside you as you connect with My mind, will, and emotion.*
>
> *Because each child of God is part of the Kingdom plan, I knit together people and groups in unity and partnership for Kingdom purposes. When two or more of my children are gathered in My Name, the kingdom is among them, multiplied.*
>
> *Again I say, the Kingdom is all centered around My will. This is why I taught you to pray.*

⁹ *"Pray, then, [a]in this way:*

'Our Father, who is in heaven,
[b]Hallowed be Your name.
10 [c]Your kingdom come,
Your [d]will be done
On earth as it is in heaven.

My Kingdom is characterized by My holiness, sovereignty, love, and righteousness. When My people reflect the Kingdom, it transforms the world!

You must be Born-again and Childlike to See it.

It is an incredible privilege to be able to see things in the spiritual realm. We don't want to take it for granted. What a gift that we have that we can encounter the Living God the way we do. In the Meet the Heavenly Father Chapter of the first book of this series we learned that childlike faith is essential to living the Christian life. Here is what Jesus taught us about that in the scriptures.

> John 3:33 Jesus answered him, "I assure you *and* most solemnly say to you, unless a person is born again [reborn from above—spiritually transformed, renewed, sanctified], he cannot [ever] see *and* experience the kingdom of God."

Seven Facts Your Authority as a Believer[12]

Some specific responsibilities go along with your authority as a believer.

1. **Jesus passed on His Power and Authority to You-** Jesus accomplished the conquering of sin and death through His

---

[12] Summarized notes from *7 Facts about your Authority as a Believer* blog article by Kenneth Copeland, 02/12/15 http://bit.ly/2Obltc8

finished work on the cross. He lived in perfect sync with the Father because He stayed tuned to His voice and exercise His power and authority through the Holy Spirit. When you accepted Christ as your Savior, you were delivered from the consequences of sin and death and you were given the authority to walk out your inheritance at that moment. All authority and power of Jesus were passed to you when the Holy Spirit came into your heart. Now you have the responsibility to steward that gift.

2. **You have the authority to preach the Gospel, Heal the Sick, Bind, Loose, and Cast out Demons** - When Jesus ascended to heaven, the body of Christ became His hands and feet. There will be proof in our lives that we are stewarding the gift of the Holy Spirit.

Matt 10:7-8 [7] And as you go, preach, saying, 'The kingdom of heaven is at hand.' [8] Heal the sick, raise the dead, cleanse the lepers, cast out demons. Freely you have received, freely give.

Matt 18:18-20 [18] I assure you *and* most solemnly say to you, whatever you bind [forbid, declare to be improper and unlawful] on earth [a]shall have [already] been bound in heaven, and whatever you loose [permit, declare lawful] on earth [b]shall have [already] been loosed in heaven.

[19] "Again I say to you, that if two [c]believers on earth agree [that is, are of one mind, in harmony] about anything that they ask [within the will of God], it will be done for them by My Father in heaven. [20] For where two or three are gathered in My name [meeting together as My followers], I am there among them."

3. **You have the authority to stand against Satan**- Satan is by no means bigger or stronger than God. You have been given

the power and the tools to stand against him. You must first recognize the enemy as your opponent. You have the authority to war in the spiritual realm and the Lord has given you the Armor of God as protection and the Sword of the Spirit as your weapon. God does not put the Armor on you or wield the Sword for you. You must put on the Armor yourself and then use the Sword with God. (See Ephesians 6:10-17)

4. **You are seated with Him in Heavenly Places with High Authority**- God has put all things under His feet. You are a member of the Body of Christ who is called to be His hands and feet. If the Lord has already put the enemy under His feet, then you need to understand and believe that God has already put the enemy under your feet by Christ Jesus. Walk out that truth in your agreement. This is how you actively are seated with Him in heavenly places. Not just when you get to heaven, but now!

Eph 1:18-23 [18] And [I pray] that the eyes of your heart [the very center and core of your being] may be enlightened [flooded with light by the Holy Spirit], so that you will know *and* cherish the [a]hope [the divine guarantee, the confident expectation] to which He has called you, the riches of His glorious inheritance in the [b]saints (God's people), [19] and [so that you will begin to know] what the immeasurable *and* unlimited *and* surpassing greatness of His [active, spiritual] power is in us who believe. These are in accordance with the working of His mighty strength [20] which He [c]produced in Christ when He raised Him from the dead and seated Him at His own right hand in the heavenly *places*, [21] far above all rule and authority and power and dominion [whether angelic or human], and [far above] every name that is named [above every title that can be conferred], not only in this age *and* world but also in the one to come. [22] And He [d]put all things [in every realm] in subjection under Christ's feet, and [e]appointed Him as [supreme and authoritative] head over all things in the church, [23] which is His body, the fullness of Him who fills *and* completes all things in all [believers].

Ephesians 2:6-7 [6] And He raised us up together with Him [when we believed], and seated us with Him in the heavenly *places*, [because we are] in Christ Jesus, [7] [and He did this] so that in the ages to come He might [clearly] show the immeasurable *and* unsurpassed riches of His grace in [His] kindness toward us in Christ Jesus [by providing for our redemption].

5. **You have the power to Exercise God's authority-** Three elements qualify you to exercise God's power and authority, miss one of them and you will not properly exercise your authority: You accepted Christ by surrendering your will to His and activated the Holy Spirit who endued you with the power, nature, and character of God, and you have the Word of God as your guide. You have the power and authority to wield the Sword of the Spirit which is the Word of God, by the power and authority of Jesus' Name, and by releasing that power by the indwelling Spirit according to God's direction. No enemy can withstand that power and authority! Know this, so you can do this!

1 Peter 1:20-23 [20] For He was [a]foreordained (foreknown) before the foundation of the world, but has appeared [publicly] in these last times for your sake [21] and through Him you believe [confidently] in God [the heavenly Father], who raised Him from the dead and gave Him glory so that your faith and hope are [centered and rest] in God.

[22] Since by your obedience to the truth you have purified yourselves for a sincere love of the believers, [see that you] love one another from the heart [always unselfishly seeking the best for one another], [23] for you have been born again [that is, reborn from above—spiritually transformed, renewed,

128

and set apart for His purpose] not of seed which is perishable but [from that which is] imperishable *and* immortal, *that is,* through the living and everlasting word of God.

6. **You have the authority to be a new creation.** – I was privileged that my dear friend and prayer partner Larry Silver, come to town to teach a local church body one Sunday. He asked the group to raise their hand if they agreed with the statement: "I am a sinner saved by grace". Nearly every hand raised. He corrected them with something to the effect of... "No, you WERE a sinner who is NOW a new creation because you were saved by Grace." I never forgot that. It is such a powerful identity truth that if grasped fully would change how you live out your Christian life.

In Romans Chapter 7 Paul goes on about what a terrible sinner he is calling himself the chief of sinners. This is the wretched man syndrome. It is when you self-identify with the sin as if it is who you are, part of your identity. Speaking this statement nullifies the truth of your actual identity in Christ. This is why I disagree with support groups that have you introduce yourself as "being the sin" even long past being delivered from it. Statements like "Hello, my name is _____ and **I am** a(n) (alcoholic, sex addict, food addict, etc)... are dangerous identity statements that make you believe you will always BE that addiction or bondage. Instead, replace this with the truths of Romans 8 which declares the power of the law of the Spirit of Life in Christ Jesus.

> Romans 8:2 For the law of the Spirit of life [which is] in Christ Jesus [the law of our new being] **has set you free** from the law of sin and of death.

A declaration that agrees with the law of the Spirit of life in Christ Jesus would be more like; "Hello, my name is _____ and I am (free, healed, whole, recovered) from (former bondage) by Jesus. The Lord has completely removed the bondage of _____ and I have been walking in victory for _____ years." Praise the Lord for His empowering yoke-breaking power! (Read ALL of Romans 8)

This is important! Speak that truth even if you are not experiencing that freedom yet, because it is the truth of your power and authority through Christ to receive it! Speaking it out loud activates it and moves you toward believing and manifesting it!

> 1 Peter 1:23 **²³ for you have been born again** [that is, reborn from above—spiritually transformed, renewed, and set apart for His purpose] not of seed which is perishable but [from that which is] imperishable *and* immortal, *that is,* through the living and everlasting word of God.

7. **You minister and release God's Love and power from a position of Authority-** Remember who and whose you are. You do not come to God as a beggar, but as His beloved child with His authority as your inheritance. Remember you minister according to what you hear and see Jesus telling you to do and say. (John 8:28). This is how Jesus did it, and this is how He commanded us to do it. When you have clearly heard Him give you an action to take, take it with authority.

I remember praying for someone once at the Cleveland House of prayer. The Lord showed me a dial with numbers from 1-10 and asked me to ask the person to rate their pain on a scale of 1-10. The person answered with the number eight. I saw that dial show eight. Then I saw Jesus twist the dial all the way to zero. I said "I see that the Lord is dialing your pain down to zero. Pain be gone in Jesus' Name!" And the person confessed that they could feel the pain lower itself until it was completely gone! I didn't beg God to do something I wanted to have to happen. He was showing me what He was already doing. I spoke in agreement with it. That's how it works!

Heb 1:3 [3] The Son is the radiance *and* only expression of the glory of [our awesome] God [reflecting God's [a] Shekinah glory, the Light-being, the brilliant light of the divine], and the exact representation *and* perfect imprint of His [Father's] essence, and upholding *and* maintaining *and* propelling all things [the entire physical and spiritual universe] by His powerful word [carrying the universe along to its predetermined goal]. When He [Himself and no other] had [by offering Himself on the cross as a sacrifice for sin] accomplished purification from sins *and* established our freedom from guilt, He sat down [revealing His completed work] at the right hand of the Majesty on high [revealing His Divine authority]

What it Looks Like to Exercise Your Authority

Here is a wonderful film clip from *The Apostle* that demonstrates a person leading a group to exercise their authority over a situation.

Film clip from The Apostle
http://bit.ly/2LWcDOw

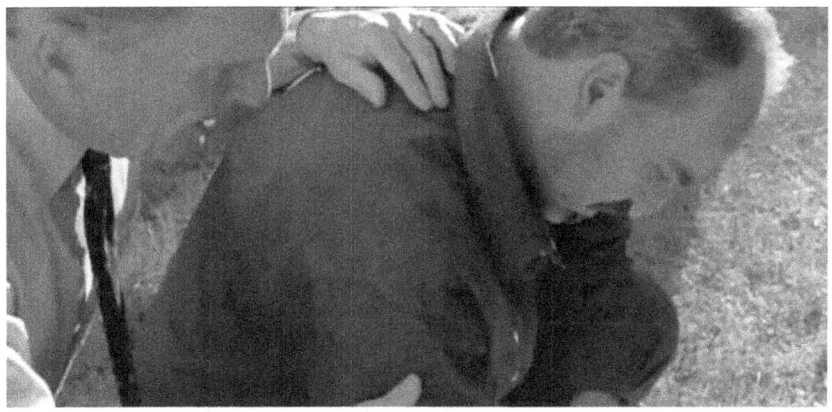

We see some amazing keys for exercising the authority of the Kingdom demonstrated in the clip. They didn't need the police or anything in the natural to rescue that church. They placed the Bible, representing God's perfect will as the line that could not be crossed. They spoke the Scriptures out loud, showing the effective use of the Sword of the Spirit, the Word of God over a circumstance. They did not beg. They declared with authority that no one would knock down that church because they knew it was God's will and nothing can go against God's will. The pastor asked the Group to say "Amen" multiple times. Amen means I agree with God. They spoke against the enemy's scheme and yet showed love and mercy to the man that was trying to execute the enemy's plan. God met that man while he was on his knees and turned around his intention. That is how it's done!

Spiritual Warfare: Battling from a Position of Authority

"Never let them see you sweat." This tagline popularized by the Dry Idea deodorant commercials in the 1980s is fitting advice when battling the enemy in spiritual warfare. Essentially the expression means to never let the opponent know you are scared. This insecure posture gives your enemy ammunition against you in a spiritual battle.

Speaking the Truth of the Word of God silences the enemy. Satan can tell if you believe what you are saying by your attitude. I have a lot of experience facilitating people to pray through the healing prayer process that was thoroughly covered in *Encountering the HEALING of God: Experience Jesus Book 2.* The casting out of the demons section of that process is the easiest step in the process because all of the contracts have been broken already by this step. The demons must leave at your command. Command. That's the key word. You don't politely ask them to leave, you *command* them to leave because they have no right to be messing with you anymore. When you believe that, they will believe that!

I remember many times getting to that phase of the process and needing to warn neighbors in an apartment complex, for example, that things would get loud. We would let them know that there would be yelling, but it's OK, it's just an exercise and no one is really in trouble except the demons!

Then when we got to that step, I would say with a loud and assertive voice... **NOW TELL THEM TO LEAVE IN JESUS NAME, THEY HAVE NO AUTHORITY HERE, THEY MUST GO NOW IN JESUS NAME!** And the person would say in the slightest of a whisper ... be gone in Jesus' name. Say it like you believe it and they will believe it too! Say it like you don't believe it and they know that you don't believe it! I would encourage people to keep saying it until their confidence in this truth backed up their words. Only then could they see the demons flee. Because the demons could see Jesus covering them when they said it! Commands according to the Truth of the Word of God are more effective and powerful than begging-type prayers without faith.

How Peter and John Did it.

Acts 3:1-8 [3] Now Peter and John were going up to the temple at the hour of prayer, the ninth hour (3:00 p.m.), [2] and a man who had been unable to walk from birth was being carried along, whom they used to set down every day at that gate of the temple which is called [a]Beautiful, so that he could beg alms from those entering the temple. [3] So when he saw Peter and John about to go into the temple, he *began* asking [them] for coins. [4] But Peter, along with John, stared at him intently and said, "Look at us!" [5] And the man *began* to pay attention to them, eagerly expecting to receive something from them. ⁶ But Peter said, "Silver and gold I do not have; but what I do have I give to you: In the name (authority, power) of Jesus Christ the Nazarene—[begin now to] walk *and* go on walking!" ⁷ Then he seized the man's right hand with a firm grip and raised him up. And at once his feet and ankles became strong *and* steady, ⁸ and with a leap he stood up and *began* to walk; and he went into the temple with them, walking and leaping and praising God.

Peter and John noticed this man because God caused them to look at him. This is how God gets your attention when there is an anointed assignment. He has you notice a person with the eyes of your heart. At that moment, Peter was seeing in the spirit what Jesus was telling Him what to do with this man. Then he commanded the man to walk by the power and authority of Jesus Christ. The man leaped to his feet and began praising God. This is how it works with us too. When God shows you or tells you what to do with someone, you can confidently pray in agreement with it and expect to see God show up!

One more thing that was interesting to me as I was studying this scripture is that I learned something significant about the Gate's name Beautiful. The Greek word for beautiful is *hóraios* which means; the hour or time of fulfillment, the beautiful timing of fruitfulness, the timing of ripeness or blooming. That crippled at-birth man had a perfect time for his healing! His purpose was to be healed and for his story to continue teaching by its inclusion in the Bible.

Spiritual Maturity is Required

God has given us all authority over **all** the power of the enemy.

Matthew 10:1 Jesus summoned His twelve disciples and gave them authority *and* power over unclean spirits, to cast them out, and to heal every kind of disease and every kind of sickness.

Luke 10: 19 [19] Listen carefully: I have given you authority [that you now possess] to tread on [a]serpents and scorpions, and [the ability to exercise authority] over **all** the power of the enemy (Satan); and nothing will [in any way] harm you.

It takes spiritual maturity to understand and even apply those truths. Most pulpits don't teach about the enemy's schemes and for sure don't encourage you to cast out demons. Yet here it is in the Bible, commanding us to do so. We must grow in spiritual maturity to be able to do what God is commanding us to do.

What is spiritual maturity? It is when you have a solid grasp of Who God is, who you are in Christ, and know the Word which is your ultimate litmus test for ensuring an accurate understanding of the first two. You cannot grow in this wisdom without having the Holy Spirit interpret the Word and having a personal relationship with Christ.

How do you do that?

Colossians 3:1-2 Therefore if you have been raised with Christ [to a new life, sharing in His resurrection from the dead], keep seeking the things that are above, where Christ is, seated at the right hand of God. [2] Set your mind *and* keep focused *habitually* on the things above [the heavenly things], not on things that are on the earth [which have only temporal value].

Your level of maturity is a factor in what the Holy Spirit will release through you. He will trust you with more when He can trust you with little.

Romans 12:2 [2] And do not be conformed to this world [any longer with its superficial values and customs], but be [a]

135

transformed *and* progressively changed [as you mature spiritually] by the renewing of your mind [focusing on godly values and ethical attitudes], so that you may prove [for yourselves] what the will of God is, that which is good and acceptable and perfect [in His plan and purpose for you].

The Word of God is the Only Weapon in the Armor

All bondage can be traced back to a lie that has somehow been agreed with. The Sword of the Spirit is the Truth that can counter the lies. (See Ephesians 6:10-17)

> Eph 6:13-17 [13] Therefore, put on the complete armor of God, so that you will be able to [successfully] resist *and* stand your ground in the evil day [of danger], and having done everything [that the crisis demands], to stand firm [in your place, fully prepared, immovable, victorious]. [14] So stand firm *and* hold your ground, HAVING [a]TIGHTENED THE WIDE BAND OF TRUTH (personal integrity, moral courage) AROUND YOUR WAIST and HAVING PUT ON THE BREASTPLATE OF RIGHTEOUSNESS (an upright heart), [15] and having [b]strapped on YOUR FEET THE GOSPEL OF PEACE IN PREPARATION [to face the enemy with firm-footed stability and the readiness produced by the good news]. [16] Above all, lift up the [protective] [c]shield of faith with which you can extinguish all the flaming arrows of the evil *one*. [17] And take THE HELMET OF SALVATION, and the sword of the Spirit, which is the Word of God.

The Armor of God protects you and the Sword of the Spirit is your weapon. There is no protection for your back because if you turn your back on God, you step outside of His umbrella of protection. If you are experiencing incredible levels of spiritual warfare, ask yourself how you may have turned your back on God's truth, or if you have not been in obedience to what He has called you.

136

Disobedience is not the only reason for experiencing spiritual warfare. Quite the opposite may be the cause. If you are bearing much fruit for the Kingdom, the enemy will try to lessen your impact with spiritual warfare. This may come in the form of an illness, lack of confidence, or attacks from others. Unfortunately, too many times these attacks come from inside the body of Christ. When I experienced this the Lord simply said, *"welcome to the club... they attacked Me too!"* Stand your ground and know that God is with you. Don't take the bait and fix your eyes on the fear of such a circumstance but find the scripture that will help you counter those lies.

In cases like this, I like to envision the Lord as a forcefield that surrounds me. When someone comes at me with accusations, I imagine this force field and only allow the truth to pierce that bubble and reach my heart. If it's true, the Lord will help me see it. Then I can confess and repent of it and He releases me from it and I move on. If it is not true, it can't hurt me. The Lord illuminates what is really behind the attack and I know better how to pray for that person or circumstance. I don't let it stop or discourage me.

How to Properly Decree and Declare

Let's begin with defining these two words. A Biblical decree is a statement that agrees with God's Word, will, and purposes. A Biblical declaration is when you speak a decree with authority over an area according to what you see and hear God directing in Jesus' Name.

Putting them together, declaring decrees is operating in the power and authority that God gave you from Jesus by speaking the Word by God's direction and command.

It is not using the Word to decree what you want to happen. You must begin with God's will related to the scripture and your circumstance. You are not the source of the power of God's will. Remember, Jesus said that apart from God, you can do nothing! (John 15:5).

Decree and declare only as the Holy Spirit instructs. Fix your eyes on Jesus, look and listen to what He is directing, and do and say only what He directs. Even Jesus lived His life doing this and we are to follow His example.

> John 12:49 [49] For I have never spoken on My own initiative *or* authority, but the Father Himself who sent Me has given Me a commandment *regarding* what to say and what to speak.

The goal is to align with God's will. Prayers that begin with our own wishes and desires don't result in miraculous outcomes. Seeking and speaking God's will does! Here is what the Lord had to say about this.

> *Too many people beg Me to do what they want Me to do, and not what I have willed for them to do. Others know the promises of My word, and bargain, beg, and plead in hope, but without faith. I need My body to rise, especially in this Kingdom season, and decree with boldness what I have already said so My Kingdom can be established on earth as it is in heaven!*
>
> *Remember to pray in Jesus' Name to seal the prayer with the power of His blood!*

Proof you are Exercising your Power and Authority

Jesus left us the Holy Spirit imparting divine authority and the power within to fulfill Kingdom purposes. Every believer can demonstrate these proofs of God's power. Mark 16 reveals Jesus' last words. They are a command to exercise His power as His hands and feet.

Mark 16:15-20 [15] And He said to them, "Go into all the world and preach the gospel to all creation. [16] He who has believed [in Me] and has been baptized will be saved [from the penalty of God's wrath and judgment]; but he who has not believed will be condemned. [17] These signs will accompany those who have believed: in My Name, they will cast out demons, they will speak in new tongues; [18] they will pick up serpents, and if they drink anything deadly, it will not hurt them; they will lay hands on the sick, and they will get well."

[19] So then, when the Lord Jesus had spoken to them, He was taken up into heaven and sat down at the right hand of God. [20] And they went out and preached everywhere, while the Lord was working with them and confirming the word by the signs that followed.

Specific Proofs

Jesus did not leave behind a powerless church. He imparted His divine authority and power of the Holy Spirit to help us accomplish the Kingdom plan. The above verse gave us a list of fruit that Jesus was looking for as active proof that you are part of His body. Are you demonstrating these things?

Leading people to Jesus- Are you sharing your faith in a way that has people want what you have? Evangelizing doesn't need to be a formal or complicated thing. Just share your story of what Jesus has meant to you and people will respond. We are called to go and make disciples. Not just to lead people to Christ, but to help them understand what that means.

Praying for people to receive the Baptism of the Holy Spirit and release the Manifestation Gifts of the Holy Spirit- Help people understand the Holy Spirit, how He works, and the full capability that people have within them because they accepted Jesus. Ananias

139

was given this specific assignment to pray for the Baptism of the Holy Spirit for Saul in Acts Chapter 9. I asked the Lord to help me understand the Baptism of the Holy Spirit.

The Baptism of the Holy Spirit is much simpler than most people make it. There are many inaccurate teachings on it. Many confuse it with the salvation prayer.

The surrendering decision of salvation deposits the seed of the Holy Spirit in the hearts of believers. The nine manifestation gifts of the Holy Spirit are like treasures hidden behind closed but unlocked doors in the heart of the believer.

The Baptism of the Holy Spirit is like watering the seed. It activates the Holy Spirit. Speaking in tongues is not the only evidence of the activation of the Holy Spirit. Any of the nine manifestations of the Holy Spirit could be activated. People could begin to prophesy, or pray for healing and see a miraculous outcome.

Activation occurs when a cry to go deeper is prayed. Seeking Me deeper triggers activation. When someone hungers for more it is a sign that they want My presence, and the Holy Spirit accommodates this heart desire. Along with it will come a desire to seek higher gifts. I want you to seek higher gifts. But I want you to seek Me even more. When you do that, the higher gifts are activated.

When you see someone hungry to go deeper, help them understand how to go deeper and pray for the Holy Spirit to release the gifts in them.

Safety from dangerous things- The Mark 16 verse above mentions snakes and poisons. It seems like a specific thing to have listed here, so I asked Jesus to explain it.

This is speaking of the promise of My divine protection. The safest place you can be is in the center of My will. You can face dangerous situations as I have unfinished assignments

*for you. Paul was shipwrecked on the Island of Malta and got
bitten by a snake and yet he was unharmed. (See Acts 28)*

*Remember that time the deer went through your windshield,
and you were unharmed? The Holy Spirit was involved in
ensuring that you and Jamael were not hurt. You both have
not finished your ministry assignments!*

Wow. How could I forget that story? My oldest daughter Jamael
was a pre-teen and would normally have been in the front seat for
this drive to pick up my other daughter from school. But on this day,
she was home doing a major homework project. A deer jumped out
from a development sign and was hit by a car going southbound.
I was approaching going north and the deer did a full tuck and
slammed through the front passenger side of the windshield and
then bounced against the empty front seat and flew out through the
broken front window onto the road directly in front of me. The whole
thing happened in slow motion. I was covered in broken glass and yet
didn't have a scratch on me.

The oddest thing about this story is where it happened. A man
was mowing his yard. He lived in the house next to that development
sign. He ran across the street to check on me and kindly invited me
inside his home until the police came. I remember telling him that my
daughter Jamael should have been in the car and that she would have
been instantly killed if she had been. That was what had me the most
shaken up.

In the ultimate case of small-world stories, that man is now
Jamael's father-in-law! It would be a few years before she and his son
would get together, and nearly seven more for them to get married.
Now we have three grandchildren that never would have existed if
the Holy Spirit hadn't ensured an unreasonable amount of homework
for Jamael that day!

Are there any close-call stories in your life? Perhaps they were also the Holy Spirit keeping you divinely protected because you have more kingdom work to accomplish!

Casting out demons- Every believer has the authority to cast out demons in Jesus' name. The steps for this are covered in the *Encountering the HEALING of God* book of this series. Once all contracts are broken, demons will leave by your command when you claim the Name of Jesus. Interestingly, they will not leave, even if contracts are broken, unless they are commanded to by Jesus' authority. Without a contract, they can't really mess with you, but they will hang around waiting for you to mess up again. In the next chapter, we will look more at the breaking of the contracts, so you know the right time to do this.

Healing the sick- It is the privilege of all believers to lay hands on the sick by Jesus' power and direction and see them recover. Having had ten miraculous healings in my own body, the Lord has allowed me to witness His miraculous healing more times now than I can count. When the Healer shows up in your life, and you get to know Him personally, He adds faith to your prayers and He releases miracles! The entire *Encountering the HEALING of God* book is dedicated to this topic.

Seeing prayers being answered- Praying in agreement with God's will is always a formula for answered prayers. God does not answer prayers in the way or in the timing that you expect.

> Hebrews 4:16 [16] Therefore let us [with privilege] approach the throne of grace [that is, the throne of God's gracious favor] with confidence *and* without fear, so that we may receive mercy [for our failures] and find [His amazing] grace to help in time of need [an appropriate blessing, coming just at the right moment].

Why People Don't Exercise their Authority

People decree things all the time. Unfortunately, they are not according to My will. They are decreeing their fears, lack of faith, and the power of their sicknesses to prevent them from doing things. They'll speak about the immensity of their trials and difficulties all agreeing with the enemy's limitations. It seems to come so naturally. That is the way of the world, not the way of My Kingdom.

Recently, Lifestyle Evangelist, Todd White was guest speaking at our church. He said; "When you woke up today, did you put on life, or did you put on Christ? Because your countenance reveals the spiritual garment that you are wearing." He went on to talk about how Moses' face shone when he came off the mountain after spending time with the Lord for 40 days. Todd urged us to have the "shiny faces" of the proof of Who we hang out with.

Lord, What specific things hold people back from exercising their power and authority? Allow His list below to act as a kind of diagnostic tool. Which of these things could be said about you?

***Lack of Faith-** The disciples cried to me asking why couldn't we drive out those demons (See Matthew 7: 19- 20). I told them that it was because of their lack of faith. Like them, many people just don't believe Me for it yet.*

***Ignorance-** Many don't understand that they have the authority to administer power. This is not well preached in the pulpits even though it is very clear in the Word of God.*

***Not in the Word-** Many are not reading the Bible with Me helping them to interpret its meaning enough to know what their inheritance is and how much power they actually have.*

***Don't believe that I still perform miracles-** Many denomi-nations teach the lie that I don't still perform miracles. This is not Biblical and negates the fact that I sent the Holy Spirit for*

143

this very purpose. Miracles can surround you every day! Many don't even acknowledge the miraculous at all, and some see miracles but do not recognize that they come from Me. This dishonors Me and weakens the Kingdom impact.

The Lie of Unworthiness- *Others agree with the lie of unworthiness. This is a false humility that has them believing that I can give authority and power to some believers but not to them. Unbelief is a form of pride making you somehow too big of a sinner for Me to be able to use. This is also not Biblical. Didn't I create all people in My image? Didn't I send the perfect Holy Spirit to dwell in each believer's heart? This lie limits My body and its Kingdom impact. Do not agree with that! Worthiness has nothing to do with it because salvation was purchased by MY worthiness, not yours.*

Fear of Man-*When you care more about what people think than what I think, you are allowing the fear of man to come in the way of your Kingdom impact. Some may persecute you for loving people enough to tell them the Truth! Welcome to the club! I need you to love Me enough to take the heat for it!*

Lack of Courage and Holy Boldness- *Many know very clearly what it is that I want them to do but hold back because of a lack of courage. Holy boldness is different than boldness. When the boldness comes from Me for you to obey something, I told you to do or say, the power to do it will be there for you. When you think the power comes from you it's easy to lack courage. Go forth in faith to heal, bring people to Salvation, cast out and trample on demons, and fulfill the purpose for which I have created you. In doing so you will do greater things than I. (See John 14: 12) This is because I am multiplied in the hearts of people exercising my power according to my authority that I pass to you.*

Lack of Spiritual Maturity- *And finally some lack the spiritual maturity to understand My nature and My Word. Without daily communion with Me, they will not grow into the maturity to understand My promises so they can boldly say and do what I ask them. Spiritually mature people know* *how to obey My voice because they know Me. They know I AM a promise keeper and that I am unable to lie. If I say something is True. It's TRUE. I AM Truth You will see My power according to the level of your wisdom, faith, trust, humility, and obedience. The more you grow in these areas the more power you will be able to release in the areas of influence for which I have given you.*

Encountering God Almighty

Remember to meet the Lord as a child and allow Him to direct the encounters. Also, beginning each encounter with doing something fun with the Lord is always a great heart-posturing exercise.

1. **Reasons for Not Exercising your Authority.** Look at the List that the Lord gave for why many don't exercise their authority and see more miraculous victories in their lives. Take note of the top 2 reasons this may be true for you and ask El Shaddai to show you how He wants you to overcome those obstacles.

2. **Superhero Side Kick-** For inspiration for this next super fun encounter with El Shaddai, watch this lyric video by Beckah Shae called *Mighty. https://youtu.be/GO4uwNSK3Sw.* After getting sufficiently pumped up, Go to the special place and take a spiritual elevator to the throne room where you will see El Shaddai dressed as the King of kings in purple and gold. He is also wearing a superhero cape. Notice that you are also wearing a superhero sidekick garment and allow Him to talk with you about how the two of you can save

the world one amazing assignment at a time! Ask Him to help you understand what it means to be seated with Him in heavenly places.

3. **The Kingdom of Heaven** - El Shaddai, help me understand more about the Kingdom of Heaven. Give me a metaphor that will help me understand the relationship between that spiritual world and this physical world.

4. **Proofs-** El Shaddai, how can I step out in faith more so I may display more proof that I am exercising my authority in the assignments that you have for me? Show a time when I have demonstrated my authority and a time when I didn't but could have.

Song: *My Fortress* by Jeremy Camp
https://youtu.be/rv7IC0FMK18

Meet the God of Justice

When I began my preparation for what would become this chapter, the Lord made it clear that this was really about Kingdom Justice. Many names of God addressed justice. The goal of this chapter is to help you understand how the legality of things works in the Kingdom of Heaven and how you can play by those rules to live out your freedom and victory in Christ.

More than one Name-

There are several roles played in the Kingdom's justice system. We will look at all of them. These names balance the truths of God's righteousness, justice, mercy, benevolence, and power. Jesus said this:

> *I want you to understand the rules of the Kingdom's justice system. The system balances the scales of justice and mercy. When you understand how it works, you can more easily pray in agreement with what I am doing and exercise your power to cooperate with it.*

Key Names of God

- **God of Justice** *Elohei Mishpat*[13]- This is a compound Name of God that includes the is-ness name of Elohei and the does-ness name *Mishpat* which means Justice. Justice is always grounded in God's omnibenevolence, love, and mercy.

    Isaiah 30:18 Therefore the LORD waits [expectantly] *and* longs to be gracious to you, And therefore He waits on high to have compassion on you. [a]For the LORD is a God of justice; Blessed (happy, fortunate) are all those who long for Him [since He will never fail them].

- **Advocate-P***araklétos*[14]- Jesus is our Advocate. The word *parakletos* means intercessor, advocate, advisor, helper, a legal advocate. He represents and counsels us much like an attorney. Jesus is the only one qualified to do this as His sacrifice made a perfect atonement for all of our sins, past, present, and future.

- **Justifier/Shield-** *Dikaioó*[15]- Jesus is also our Justifier. He is our replacement program. He doesn't defend our sins, He covers them completely. The word *dikaioó* means to make righteous, defend the cause of, plead for the righteousness (innocence) of, acquit, and justify; hence: I regard it as righteous. He is our shield. Ephesians 6, states that the shield of faith is part of our armor of protection. This means that our belief in Jesus is key to Him being our shield. We must put on faith to experience Him as our shield.

- **Witnesses-** *ud, martus*- There are 139 verses related to the term witness which essentially means an eye or an ear witness.

---

[13] Biblehub.com Lexicon search for Isaiah 30:18, search words God of Justice
[14] Biblehub.com search concordance 3875 *parakletos* search word advocate
[15] Biblehub.com search concordance 1344 *dikaioó* search word justifier.

150

The word *martus* means to personally see and hear something so that it can be testified about in a court of law. One constant witness is the Lord whose omnipresent eye sees and hears all things.

- **Judge of All- *El Shaphat*[16]-** This Name refers to the God of Judgement at the end of all days. For the believer, judgment is not about punishment, but our measure of reward. As you can see, *El Shaphat* is another compound name. *El* refers to the fullness of who God IS, and *Shaphat* means the God who executes judgment, like a judge who rules on a case.

How it Works in a Natural Courtroom

The key players in an earthly courtroom are the Judge, the lawyers, the defendants, the prosecutors, the witnesses for both parties and in some cases the jurors.

Whether you have ever been in a courtroom personally or not, you have likely watched some court-related programming to have a context for how things work in a court situation. Evidence is presented on both sides facilitated by legal teams. The desired outcome is justice being served and a closed case.

The entire process is held together by laws and systems for interpreting them. So many things on earth are mere shadows of what goes on in heaven.

Systems for Truth in the Kingdom of Heaven

You are a citizen of heaven. This means that you are subject to the laws of the Kingdom as well as the ones on earth.

---

[16] Biblehub.com lexicon Psalm 75:7 key words searched God of Judgement.

- **Law- Word of God- Sword of Defense-** Jesus perfectly fulfills the law and because He lives inside of you, the law is within you. The inner wisdom of God's will is accessible to you.

  Matthew 5:17-19 [17] "Do not think that I came to do away with or undo the [a]Law [of Moses] or the [writings of the] Prophets; I did not come to destroy but to fulfill. [18] For I assure you and most solemnly say to you, until heaven and earth pass away, not the smallest letter or stroke [of the pen] will pass from the Law until all things [which it foreshadows] are accomplished. [19] So whoever breaks one of the least [important] of these commandments, and teaches others to do the same, will be called least [important] in the kingdom of heaven; but whoever practices and teaches them, he will be called great in the kingdom of heaven.

- **Covenants and Contracts-** The word for covenant in the bible is *diatheke* which means; a will, a testament, a set agreement having complete terms determined by the initiating party and confirmed by the one entering into the covenant.

God is a promise-keeping God and desires His people to be covenant-keeping like Him. Covenants are created to be forever promises. When you accept the Lord into your heart, for example, you are sealed until the day of redemption. No one can snatch you from God's hands! (See John 10:28)

  Hebrews 8:10 For this is the covenant that I will make with the house of Israel
  After those days, says the Lord:
  I will imprint My laws upon their minds [even upon their innermost thoughts and understanding],
  And engrave them upon their hearts [effecting their regeneration].

152

And I will be their God,
And they shall be My people.

So we see in this verse that we have within our hearts when we are believers that the imprint of God's law is accessible to us to the innermost thoughts and understanding. This is accomplished by the indwelling Holy Spirit.

Contracts are intended to be temporary. They are set up with certain conditions, that when met, end the agreement. A real estate agreement is an example of a contract. When all of the pre-determined conditions are met, the property moves into a new person's ownership, and the relationship between seller and buyer is completed. Marriage is designed by God to be a covenantal relationship, although many people think of it as a contract.

> Isaiah 28:18 Your covenant with death will be annulled, And your agreement with Sheol (the place of the dead) will not stand; When the overwhelming scourge passes through, Then you will become its trampling ground.

- **Agreement- Who and to what are you agreeing?** Whether you realize it or not, you are always agreeing with something. Your behaviors reveal those things for which your heart is agreeing.

The Lord gives much advice about this in the Word;

> Colossians 2:8 See to it that no one takes you captive through philosophy and empty deception [pseudo-intellectual babble], according to the tradition [and musings] of mere men, following the [a]elementary principles of this world, rather than following [the truth—the teachings of] Christ.

Romans 12:2 And do not be conformed to this world [any longer with its superficial values and customs], but be [a] transformed and progressively changed [as you mature spiritually] by the renewing of your mind [focusing on godly values and ethical attitudes], so that you may prove [for yourselves] what the will of God is, that which is good and acceptable and perfect [in His plan and purpose for you].

Agreements with anything that is not from God open the door for the enemy by allowing legitimate contracts to mess with you. The contracts are in place only when you agree with them. Confessing and repenting of the limiting lying thoughts and destructive behaviors break the contracts with the enemy. Guard your heart!

- **Witnesses and Testimony-** Eye and ear witnesses are anyone who has seen and heard the truth. One key witness is your Omnipresent LORD. He has seen and heard everything you have ever done and was present for every interaction you have ever had. He is also Omniscient, He knows everything.

You are also a witness and testify for or against yourself by your own words and behaviors. You need to know the Truth so He can set you free. Not agreeing that you have played a role in certain challenging issues and relationships can keep you in bondage. Victimization is an effective strategy of the enemy, keeping your eyes on your offenses and offenders keeps them off of God and limit your awareness of what you may need to confess and repent of to heal relationships.

Psalm 139:23 Search me [thoroughly], O God, and know my heart; Test me and know my anxious thoughts; 24 And see if there is any wicked or hurtful way in me, And lead me in the everlasting way.

A third category of witnesses is other people, organizations, and institutions. What are people saying about me? What true evidence can be found by these witnesses? Is this evidence God honoring or does it reveal true issues for which I need to confess or repent? Or is this testimony false?

The enemy testifies against you when you have given him a legitimate contract when you sin or when your words don't agree with God.

> Colossians 1:16 For [a]by Him all things were created in heaven and on earth, [things] visible and invisible, whether thrones or dominions or rulers or authorities; all things were created and exist through Him [that is, by His activity] and for Him.

Some great questions to ask the Lord related to these witnesses and their testimony are:

- Lord, what have I been agreeing with that has allowed the enemy to have a contract to mess with me?

- Lord, what has been my confession related to this issue? Am I agreeing with the truth of your Word and speaking faith, hope, and love? Or am I agreeing with the enemy and have been agreeing with fear, hate, malice, or hopelessness?

- Lord, who else is testifying against me? What people, organizations, or institutions have railed against me? Show me the truth, Lord. Is there anything I need to confess or repent of now, or do I need to forgive and release them because they don't understand what they are doing?

The Blood of Jesus

Understanding the Power of Jesus' Blood
https://youtu.be/8Z_SMrnEiaI

There are three things that all blood does: It is lifegiving, it cleanses, and it heals. In the natural world, we cannot live without blood. Blood gives life to all parts of the body.

> Leviticus 17:14 For regarding the life of all flesh, its blood is [the same] as its life; therefore I said to the Israelites, 'You are not to eat the blood of any flesh, for the [a]life of all flesh is its blood. Whoever eats it shall be cut off [excluding him from the atonement made for them].

The job of the blood is to carry away waste and filth, purifying us from what would naturally kill us. In this manner, it cleanses. When you have a cut, the body uses the blood to coagulate and heal the wound.

In the Old Testament days, blood sacrifices by perfect animals were required to atone for our sins. Animals needed to be without blemish and the atonement was temporary. These sacrifices needed to be done over and over to manage the sin of the people.

156

Jesus' blood is supernatural and is perfectly life-giving, cleansing, and healing for us spiritually.

> 1 Peter 2:24 He personally carried our sins in His body on the [a]cross [willingly offering Himself on it, as on an altar of sacrifice], so that we might die to sin [becoming immune from the penalty and power of sin] and live for righteousness; for by His wounds you [who believe] have been [b]healed.

> Hebrews 9:14 how much more will the blood of Christ, who through the eternal [Holy] Spirit willingly offered Himself unblemished [that is, without moral or spiritual imperfection as a sacrifice] to God, cleanse your conscience from dead works and lifeless observances to serve the ever-living God?

As believers in Christ, Jesus has given us a heavenly blood transfusion. His blood that was sacrificed to purchase your eternal life mingles with your blood, empowering you to be cleansed, to live, and to be healed. Realizing that truth and living out the understanding of it is the journey of the Christian life and your path to your Christ-Identity.

Because of Jesus' victorious resurrection, you have a new birth, a new life with an inheritance you can live out of now. This new life never spoils, and can never perish or fade. But you must realize it and live out of that truth to experience it.

The Father sees you and Jesus together in a perfected Christ-You. The enemy sees you as you see yourself. If you see yourself as anything less than your true inherited self, the enemy can work with that!

What is your full inheritance? Here are five things that you have now because of the blood of Jesus!

1. Redemption

Ephesians 1:7 In Him we have redemption [that is, our deliverance and salvation] through His blood, [which paid the penalty for our sin and resulted in] the forgiveness *and* complete pardon of our sin, in accordance with the riches of His grace.

2. Fellowship with God

Hebrews 10:19 In Him we have redemption [that is, our deliverance and salvation] through His blood, [which paid the penalty for our sin and resulted in] the forgiveness *and* complete pardon of our sin, in accordance with the riches of His grace

3. Healing

Isaiah 53:5 But He was wounded for our transgressions, He was crushed for our wickedness [our sin, our injustice, our wrongdoing]; The punishment [required] for our well-being *fell* on Him, And by His stripes (wounds) we are healed.

4. Protection

Exodus 12:13 The blood shall be a sign for you on [the doorposts of] the houses where you live; when I see the blood I shall pass over you, and no affliction shall happen to you to destroy you when I strike the land of Egypt.

5. Authority over the devil

Revelation 12:11 The blood shall be a sign for you on [the doorposts of] the houses where you live; when I see the blood I shall pass over you, and no affliction shall happen to you to destroy you when I strike the land of Egypt.

The Courts of Heaven

Robert Henderson has written many books on the Courts of Heaven. He has been ministering a process of healing and deliverance through a legal process that addresses spiritual issues in the Kingdom. Many testify to its effectiveness in helping them find healing and justice. I asked the Lord to help me understand this process.

> Lord, are the Courts of Heaven a metaphor or creative tool to help identify spiritual issues and facilitate the application of Your blood to our circumstances or are there legitimate heavenly realm(s) that operate as Courts of Heaven?

> *This is not the right question. The more important distinction is that it is a real process that works because it is facilitated by Me and applies My blood to issues. Nothing can overcome My blood. This question is not one of those theological issues that are worth fighting over.*

> *It is not the only path to justice, but it is an effective one! It is a helpful way to understand how I balance My justice and mercy. The most important thing for you to understand is how and why you allow the enemy to obtain contracts against you and how to allow ME to take care of them with you.*

> *It is also important to understand the role of My Blood, so you know how to apply it to all circumstances. Like any other encounter we have designed in this book, it works because it is in cooperation with Me and executes My will for healing and justice.*

> *Visualizing ME is what is important. Seeing Me as your Defender in the Court Room, applying the Blood, and understanding the power of the blood is key. Innocence is determined by applying My perfect innocence to you. This is the truth of the New Covenant. The Father sees you and I united uniquely with My perfection covering you.*

It is also important in this process to see yourself on the other side of the courtroom. How are you nullifying My work on the cross by agreeing with the lies of the enemy? This process helps you see this in a dynamic courtroom setting. It will help you catch yourself when you agree with lies and help you claim the Truth of your Christ-Identity.

Ultimately, the Courts of Heaven experience shows you how to apply your legitimate authority over the enemy by the power of My blood so you can stay free.

God's Justice System

The courts of heaven process can seem extremely complicated. Henderson has charts and graphs and loads of different courts you could appeal to in his many books and training courses on this topic. I will do my best to make this as simple as possible to make the point of another creative way that you can find healing, deliverance, and freedom with God.

If you read Encountering the HEALING of God; Experience Jesus Book 2, you learned how spiritual healing works and how to receive healing. The courts of heaven process are similar in so many ways. They are both about identifying the areas in your life that do not align or agree with God's perfect plan. In the healing process, we learned that many issues that we have in life are because we agreed with the enemy and not with God. So the process is similar in that it identifies the areas for which you have given the enemy a contract to mess with you.

The original contract that the enemy received was from Adam and Eve's original sin. Their sin put a curse on all of us and gave the enemy legitimate authority to tempt and menace people, as long as you give them a legitimate reason. It is important to understand that the enemy is under God Almighty's sovereign control. Satan and his minions cannot attack you without the permission you give them by legitimate contracts. Contracts are given by sin, curses, and anyway in which you behave outside of God's will.

However, Jesus accomplished the reverse of that curse on the cross. By living a sinless life and defeating death and the grave Jesus became your covering, your advocate, and by the power of His blood you can come boldly into the throne room and any of the courts of heaven and plead your cases, and 100% of the time, receive not guilty verdicts because of the covering of Jesus' blood.

Types of Cases to Bring to the Court

Once you are saved, Satan cannot rob you of your heavenly destiny. The only thing he can do is rob you of your kingdom impact. Because courts of heaven are about justice, your defense must be related to your kingdom purpose. For example, If you have been given prophetic promises to accomplish certain things in this life for God, and you have been given a terminal diagnosis, You can come to the court with your unfinished calling as your defense.

I recently heard a story about Kim Clement at the beginning of his ministry career. The Lord had given him huge prophetic promises that he would evangelize and disciple specific nations. He was on an airplane that had a dramatic 1000-foot drop because it hit an air pocket. People were panicking and screaming, some others were praying and crying.

Kim Clement stood in the aisle and started shouting; "China, India, the United States..."

Then suddenly things settled down, and the pilot assured people that the plane was fine, and it would not happen again. The person sitting next to Kim Clement asked him what he was doing. And he answered something like: "The Lord gave me some promises and I was simply reminding Him what they were." Kim knew that it was not his time because of these promises. And he was declaring that truth out loud as a mighty prayer warrior strategy.

The court of Heaven experience is similar to this. It's when the books of your destiny are examined and when the blood of Jesus is applied to all circumstances. It is a method of visualizing Jesus as your Advocate representing you to the Father and covering you with the blood that pays for all your transgressions.

Just like in regular courtrooms, there are defendants, prosecutors, and witnesses. The court of heaven is an encountering experience where you see the enemy's case against you and you can respond to the testimony of the witnesses by either repenting for true convictions, denouncing condemnations from the enemy that are lies, and countering them with the truth of God's word.

Next, ask the Lord what other conditions would need to be met for all agreements with the enemy to be broken. Obey the conditions that the God of Justice identifies. Agree with all those conditions, and see Jesus apply the blood over your case.

Presenting your Case in the Courts of Heaven

It is important to visualize Jesus in this courtroom, and just as if you were a defendant in any courtroom, you need to trust Jesus as your Defender and follow His lead. Jesus knows how to guide you through it. So allow Him to do that. Begin by imagining a courtroom with Jesus, seeing Him, the angels and the Heavenly Father present there. Allow Jesus to take the lead.

Witnesses and Testimony

Throughout the entire Bible, we see a pattern similar to a court of law. Many Greek and Hebrew words for God, Jesus, and the Holy Spirit will confirm the roles of the lawgiver, advocate, intercessor, and witness.

There are many verses in the Bible about this—and I encourage you to search them out. I've provided a few verses below to illustrate the "roles" of "who does what" in the Courts of Heaven:

- We are Petitioners-Philippians 4:6 NIV Do not be anxious about anything, but in every situation, by prayer and petition, with thanksgiving, present your requests to God.

- Other Witnesses- In addition to others with whom you are having conflicts, you are nearly always testifying against yourself as well. It is a strange thing to be standing with Jesus on one side of the courtroom and see yourself standing with Satan on the other aisle. This is because your words and actions have issued the contract in the first place. The enemy will point out your self-deprecating, self-limiting statements, your acts of disobedience, and your sinful patterns.

- The Lord is our judge- Isaiah 33:22 NIV God is our Judge (but not a judge as you might think; remember God is also a loving Father and is not out to judge you!): For the Lord is our judge, the Lord is our lawgiver, the Lord is our king; it is he who will save us.

- Jesus is our Mediator (attorney)- 1 Timothy 2:5 NIV For there is one God and one mediator between God and mankind, the man Christ Jesus.

- Holy Spirit is our Witness: Romans 8:16 NIV The Spirit himself testifies with our spirit that we are God's children.

- Satan is our Prosecutor: Revelation 12:10b NIV For the accuser of our brothers and sisters, who accuses them before our God day and night, has been hurled down.

- Angels are also present in the courtroom, ministering to your needs as Jesus directs.

Responding to the Testimony

- **Repent for true convictions.** If your sin has contributed to this issue, take responsibility for it by confessing and repenting.

- **Denounce condemnations from the enemy or those speaking on his behalf.** Lies need to be identified and contrasted with the Truth from the word of God.

- **What agreements/contracts need to be broken?** Ask this question, and Jesus will let you know what the open doors were to allow the enemy to mess with you.

- **Change your agreement-** Apply the Scripture that will set you free.

See Jesus accomplish it with you...

- **Allow Jesus to be your Shield/Justifier-** Speak in agreement with the scriptures and see yourself blanketed or otherwise covered by Jesus' perfection.

  - **Apply the Blood with the authority of Jesus' Name-** This will look different for everyone. Speak in agreement with the authority you have out loud.

- **Hear the Ruling from the God of Justice-** Close the Case and walk in Freedom!

Case Example

In this case example is from an anonymous woman who knew nothing at all about the courts of heaven. The Lord simply showed up as her Defender in a real legal circumstance.

> I was going through the divorce process with my husband of 19 years. I had tried to hold this off for many years, but it was no longer possible. I was working in the insurance section of a large hospital. The pay was modest, the benefits were great, and the job was stressful.
>
> My attorney had told me that the main reason for the deposition was to see if I could be rattled and make a poor witness on the stand. If so, they would hold a court case instead of settling so that he wouldn't have to pay alimony. On the day of the deposition, I worked my usual hours, from 7:00 am to 3:30 pm then ran to my car and got to the attorney's office as quickly as I could. I was exhausted because I had had so little sleep the night before. Also, I hadn't had time to eat lunch and I could feel the shakiness of my blood sugar level dropping. Worse, was the thought of facing the hatred and anger my husband had built up that he was now unleashing toward me. I parked my car in the gray and cold rain. I remember putting both of my hands at the top of the steering wheel and leaning forward with my forehead on the back of my hands. "Jesus, I have nothing. I don't feel well. I have nothing in me. Please help me."
>
> I went into a very impressive conference room with a long table. At the side of one end sat my husband and his attorney.
>
> Across the table sat my attorney and her boss which concerned me. Why both? What was going to happen here? The court reporter was set up at the end of the table and I sat to her left, across from my husband's attorney.
>
> As soon as we started, something came over me. It had to be the Holy Spirit. I was calm, poised, engaged, and forthright

165

with good eye contact and every answer was short, honest, and clever enough to expose the truth without saying anything negative about my husband. I saw and heard myself speak but I could hardly believe it was me! All the while, my husband was not allowed to speak to me or his attorney, but he wrote fiendishly on a legal pad as though stabbing it with a knife.

We took a recess after 2 hours. In the elevator, my attorneys turned to me shocked. This was the first time either of them had seen me when I wasn't in tears. I said to them, "This isn't me; you're seeing God at work." They weren't comfortable with that answer, but it was the truth.

We went back in to continue the deposition and it was the same. But now, while this was going on - even while I was talking, I had a vision of a large table behind me that had, not the accusations of my husband, but my real sins piled on it. I saw Jesus standing in front of it with his back to the table with my lifetime of sins. His arms spread out to each side, at a downward angle so that the fingertips of each hand touched the edge of the table behind him. And in my vision, Jesus said, "Not guilty". The vision stayed with me until the end of the deposition. I continued to answer questions in the same way, but the vision was there for me.

I still have the transcript of that deposition. But I'll never forget Jesus showing up for me in my weakness. It is one of the best days of my life.

P.S. My ex-husband seems to have worked through his rage and returned to his faith.

Encountering the God of Justice

Remember to meet the Lord as a child and allow Him to direct the encounters. Also, beginning each encounter with doing something fun with the Lord is always a great heart-posturing exercise.

1. **My Open Doors-** Lord, where have I opened a door and given the enemy a contract to mess with me by any words or actions that I have taken? What is the case against me? Then, confess and repent anything that the Lord reveals to you and ask Him what to do as your next step.

2. **Evidence For or Against-** If a typical day in your life could be viewed as evidence in the court of heaven, would you be testifying in favor of your defense or the prosecution? Ask the Lord to show you your heart to reveal if you daily tend to agree more with the enemy or more with God. Ask the Lord to speak to you about how you can more habitually see things from His perspective.

3. **Witness and Testify!** Lord, show me some simple and practical ways I can share what I have experienced personally with you so I may boldly proclaim how real, powerful, and transformational you are in my life. How can I use my life's stories to persuade others to trust You too?

4. **Take your Case to the Court of Heaven-** Ask the Lord Jesus your Advocate to identify an area for which you are struggling and have fallen out of agreement with His perfect will and you would like to have Jesus, your Advocate represent you in this case, Have Jesus take you to the Court of Heaven.

Have a conversation with Jesus and allow Him to show you the lie that you have to replace with the Truth from the Word of God.

See *El Shaphat* sitting as the Judge, the Enemy, and any witnesses that he has on the left side of the courtroom, Jesus standing with you and your witnesses on the right side of the courtroom.

As the Enemy makes His case against you,

See Jesus as your covering as He only allows TRUTH and combats the lies of the enemy. Confess and repent of any sin for which you are guilty and ask the Lord for forgiveness. Forgive yourself, God, and anyone else who was involved in the lie besetting your heart. Reject any lies of the enemy with the Scripture that counters it. (Jesus will help you with this part!)

Speak with Jesus in an authoritative tone, say: "I apply the Blood of Jesus, that nothing can overcome and by the power of your Word, Jesus Christ to this situation. Having confessed and repented, and sought forgiveness, I now break any agreements previously held by the enemy in this area. All contracts are now null and void!"

Then at that command look and see the Blood of Jesus come like a river from the back of the courtroom, flowing and covering over your head and the pile of evidence, instantly dissolving it. Feel the release of the guilt lift as Jesus takes on this and releases it forever.

Turn to those who were involved in any false accusations and pray a prayer of forgiveness and blessing over them. If they are not saved, pray for their salvation.

Hear the gavel slam as the God of Justice declares you not guilty and closes the case. Give Jesus Thanks and Praise. Celebrate with Him by doing something really fun!

For more detailed instructions on how to take a case to the Courts of Heaven, see Appendix D at the back of this book.

Whom Shall I Fear [God of the Angel Armies] by Chris Tomlin
https://youtu.be/R0gu0nOaFsI

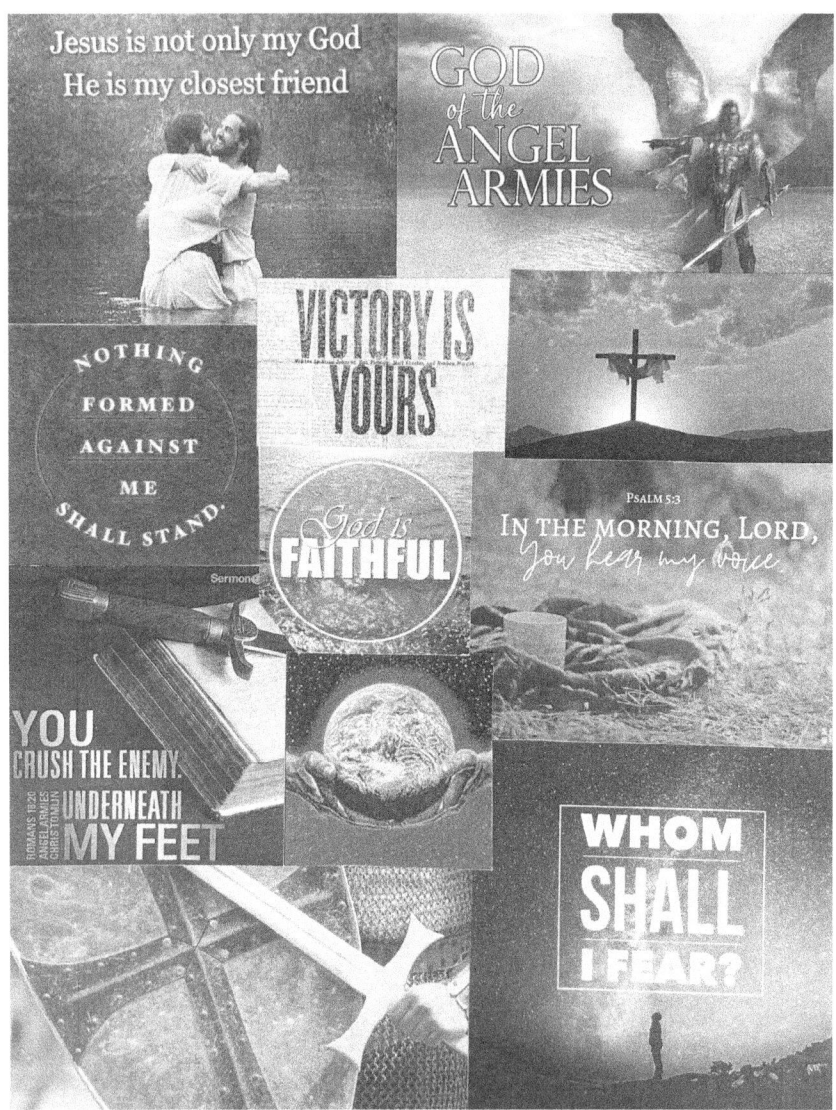

Meet the LORD of Hosts

⎯⎯⎯⎯⎯

*J*ehovah Saboath is the name for the God of Warfare, Chief of the Angel Armies. He is known by several names including the LORD of Hosts, the LORD of the Angel Armies, and in the Old Testament, Jesus Himself shows up pre-incarnate as The Angel of the LORD.

There are 273 verses referencing the LORD of Hosts in the Amplified translation. Most are in Isaiah with 60 incidences, and Zechariah with 46 incidences. When you see the all-caps LORD or Jehovah we know that this is referring to the fullness of all that God is and *Saboath* means angel armies.

Generally looking at the first seven chapters of Zechariah, we see the LORD of Hosts saving His people from their adversaries and fighting jealously for them. He protects those who are obedient to His commands and clearly communicates how to stay under His protection by reminding the people of His commands and statutes. There is a justice side to this name as He warns people when they are going off track and calls them to repentance.

In the latter chapters of Zechariah, we see the prophetic nature of the LORD of Hosts. In chapters 8-14 we see Him anoint and empower prophets and He shares end-time prophetic revelation. His goal is always to dispense judgment with love and mercy, consistent with His nature and character.

There are 53 verses referencing The Angel of the LORD and in the AMP version. The incidences show stories of preserving the destiny of the Kingdom plan. The Angel of the LORD showed up to encourage Hagar that she and her son Ishmael would survive and he would become the father of many nations. Baalam encountered The Angel of the LORD when He caused the donkey to see Him on the road with a drawn sword to stop him from disobeying God's plan.

Moses received the promise and purposes of the future of Israel from The Angel of the LORD speaking to him from the burning bush. David and Gideon were given direction and angel warrior assistance from battles directed by The Angel of the LORD.

Understanding Angels

Angels were created by God to serve Him and His people. They are spiritual beings that live eternally. We know that they were present when the Lord created the earth as in Job chapter 38, the Lord asks Job if he was there when He created the earth and the angels were shouting with Joy.

Angels do not have any Omni abilities. They are not all-powerful or everywhere present like God, for example. They have free will and we know that two-thirds of them remained faithful to God when the others rebelled and were cast out of heaven.

Types of Good Angels

There are many types of angels and more heavenly beings that we will address in this chapter. The Seraphim and Cherubim are angels who appear to only be in the Throne room of heaven ministering to God directly. [17]

Seraphim

The word seraph means burning ones. The seraphim are considered the highest order of angels. The seraphim are described in detail by Isaiah and John. (See Revelation 4)

> Isaiah 6:1-7 In the year that King Uzziah died, I saw [in a vision] the Lord sitting on a throne, high and exalted, with the train of His royal robe filling the [most holy part of the] temple. ² Above Him seraphim (heavenly beings) stood;

each one had six wings: with two *wings* he covered his face, with two *wings* he covered his feet, and with two *wings* he flew. [3] And one called out to another, saying,

"Holy, Holy, Holy is the Lord of hosts; The whole earth is filled with His glory."

[4] And the foundations of the thresholds trembled at the voice of him who called out, and the temple was filling with smoke. [5] Then I said,

"Woe is me! For I am ruined, Because I am a man of [ceremonially] unclean lips, And I live among a people of unclean lips; For my eyes have seen the King, the Lord of hosts."

[6] Then one of the seraphim flew to me with a burning coal in his hand, which he had taken from the altar with tongs. [7] He touched my mouth *with it* and said, "Listen carefully, this has touched your lips; your wickedness [your sin, your injustice, your wrongdoing] is taken away and your sin atoned for *and* forgiven."

We learn from these verses that the primary role of the seraphim is to worship the LORD. They may be considered to be made of fire or shine brightly because of their constant proximity to the Glory of God. Additionally, the seraph in this verse example had the high delegated authority to cleanse Isaiah of his sins. This was important because he was standing in the very Presence of God Almighty. This was not necessary for John as his sins were already forgiven by the finished work of Jesus Christ.

I have no idea why many artists have depicted cherubim as chubby-winged babies. Their actual appearance is nothing like this! There are 60 verses in the Bible about cherubim with only one in the New Testament. The top 3 books referencing them are Ezekiel, Exodus, and 1 Kings with 20, 11, and 11 verses respectively. The most detailed descriptions are in Ezekiel. (See Ezekiel 1) and (Revelation 4)

This angelology video by Artist Tim Gagnon does a great job of explaining that there are different types of cherubim and although it seemed like they were seeing the same cherubim, John and Ezekiel actually saw different kinds of cherubim.

Cherubim

https://youtu.be/MvU3_GZOyLM[18]

The Lord revealed to me that the faces represent the nature and glory of God with the face of the eagle representing God's omnipresence able to see everything from His highest vantage point. The face of the ox represents God's omnipotence/strength. The face of the Lion, His omniscience/wisdom, and the face of the man his omnibenevolence as man is made in His image and character.

Messengers

The word angel means messenger. Gabriel is the most well-known of the angels dispatched to share really important messages as they

---

[18] Tim Gagnon angelology video *Cherubim www.youtube.com/watch?v=MvU3_GZOyLM*

relate to God's plans. Daniel had several encounters with Gabriel in Daniel chapters 8, 9, 10, and 11. Gabriel was sent to help Daniel understand his visions about the upcoming messiah and the end times of the world.

Gabriel shows up in the New Testament when he informs Zacharias that he and his wife will have a baby who would grow up to be John the Baptist. Then again he shows up to inform Mary of God's plan for her to carry and bring the Messiah into the world.

Warriors

Michael is known as an archangel or a prince. An archangel is a top-ranking warrior angel. He happens to be the archangel of Israel. Each nation has its own archangels. The Lord revealed to me that the archangel for the United States is named Liberty. Warrior angels fight against the enemy in unseen battles all the time.

By name, Michael is mentioned nine times in the Bible. In Revelation chapter 12 we learn of a war being waged in heaven with the dragon. Gabriel shares with Daniel what Michael is doing to fight and rescue Israel and all those whose names are in the Book of Life.

Daniel 12:1 "Now at that [end] time Michael, the great [angelic] prince who stands *guard* over the children of your people, will arise. And there will be a time of distress such as never occurred since there was a nation until that time; but at that time your people, everyone who is found written in the Book [of Life], will be rescued.

Guardians

Watchers, also known as guardians, are the angels that are assigned to every person to watch and care for their needs.

Psalm 91:11 For He will command His angels in regard to you, To protect *and* defend *and* guard you in all your ways [of obedience and service].

God is a God of order. There is a hierarchy related to the angels. Seraphim and Cherubim serve God in the throne room at the highest level. Archangels are over Nations. Guardians are over individuals and there are levels in between called thrones, principalities, and dominions. Each with its own roles and levels of responsibility.

Good Angel Nature and Character

Because angels dwell in the presence of the LORD, they reflect God by His nature and character. They express emotions of the Fruit of the Spirit; love, joy, peace, patience, gentleness, goodness, faithfulness, and self-control. (See Galatians 5:22-23) Joy is the number one characteristic associated with angels in the bible.

Angels are spiritual beings and can look like anything they need to look like. They can and often do manifest as people. Some have been seen with wings and others without wings. Some can look like children and others like mighty giant warriors.

We have no idea how many angels there are because they are uncountable. Psalm 68 says there are myriads and myriads of angels. Myriad means innumerable, countless. We do know that two-thirds of the angels chose to stay with God. Angels were created to serve and love to be of service!

Fallen Angels/Demons

We do not know when angels were created or the full story of the rebellion that was spearheaded by Lucifer, a high-ranking cherub angel that was supposed to be the most beautiful of angels. He was considered a prince, so likely at the archangel level. We know that pride was the culprit.

> Ezekiel 28:12b-17 'Thus says the Lord GOD, "You had the full measure of perfection *and* the finishing touch [of completeness], Full of wisdom and perfect in beauty. [13] "You were in [a]Eden, the garden of God; Every precious stone was your covering: The ruby, the topaz, and the diamond; The beryl, the onyx, and the jasper; The lapis lazuli, the turquoise, and the emerald; And the gold, the workmanship of your [b]settings and your sockets, was in you. They were prepared on the day that you were created.

> [14] "You were the anointed cherub who covers *and* protects, And I placed you there. You were on the holy mountain of God; You walked in the midst of the stones of fire [sparkling jewels].[15] "You were blameless in your ways from the day you were created until unrighteousness *and* evil were found in you. [16] "Through the abundance of your commerce you were internally filled with lawlessness *and* violence, and you sinned; Therefore I have cast you out as a profane *and* unholy thing from the mountain of God. And I have destroyed you, O covering cherub, From the midst of the stones of fire. [17] "Your heart was proud *and* arrogant because of your beauty; You destroyed your wisdom for the sake of your splendor. I cast you to the ground; I lay you before kings, that they might look at you.

I asked the Lord how some angels become fallen angels and others stay faithful. This was His response:

> *All created angels were given free will. Some came down to earth and joined with women, creating the Nephalim, the race of superhuman giants.*

> Genesis 6:1-7 Now it happened, when men began to multiply on the face of the land, and daughters were born

to them, **2** that the [ᵃ]sons of God saw that the daughters of men were beautiful *and* desirable; and they took wives for themselves, whomever they chose *and* desired. **3** Then the LORD said, "My Spirit shall not strive *and* remain with man forever, because he is indeed flesh [sinful, corrupt— given over to sensual appetites]; nevertheless his days shall yet be [ᵇ]a hundred and twenty years." **4** There were Nephilim (men of stature, notorious men) on the earth in those days—and also afterward—when the sons of God lived with the daughters of men, and they gave birth to their *children*. These were the mighty men who were of old, men of renown (great reputation, fame).

5 The LORD saw that the wickedness (depravity) of man was great on the earth, and that every imagination *or* intent of the thoughts of his heart were only evil continually. **6** The LORD [ᶜ]regretted that He had made mankind on the earth, and He was [deeply] grieved in His heart. **7** So the LORD said, "I will destroy (annihilate) mankind whom I have created from the surface of the earth—not only man, but the animals and the crawling things and the birds of the air—because it [deeply] grieves Me [to see mankind's sin] *and* I regret that I have made them."

Jesus said this;

The sons of God in this verse refer to angels. So angels married women and had children, the Nephilim. These are the people that are talked about in ancient Greek Mythology, selfish and powerful giants. They abandoned their heavenly dwelling place and came to earth to steal, kill and destroy.

Jude 1:6-7 **⁶** And angels who did not keep their own designated place of power, but abandoned their proper dwelling place, [these] He has kept in eternal chains under [the thick gloom of utter] darkness for the judgment of the great day, **⁷** just as Sodom and Gomorrah and the adjacent cities, since they in the same way as these *angels* indulged in gross immoral freedom *and* unnatural vice and sensual perversity. They are exhibited [in plain sight] as an example of undergoing the punishment of everlasting fire.

Jesus clarified;

> *Other angels had this heart posture. Because I live in timelessness and am Omni-present and Omniscient, I knew which were rebellious and which were faithful. The rebellious were cast away from heaven and the faithful remain with Me in heaven.*

> *All are under My authority. Satan and his demons only have the authority to tempt people by the free will decisions of mankind. They are not more powerful than Me. The end of their story is already written. (See* Revelation 12:7-17)

What Angels Do

I had the privilege of attending a presentation by Dr. Charity Virkler Kayembe where she summarized fifteen things that the angels do for us. She had researched the 365 scriptures referencing angels in the Bible for her book *Everyday Angels* that she co-wrote with Joe Brock and her presentation shared this list and scripture context. It is here for you with a couple more I found in my research for this book.

What they do	Scripture	Bible Story Context
Worship and praise the Lord	(Isaiah 6:3)	Throne room
Guards us	(Psalm 91:11-12)	God shares this purpose for angels
Deliver prophetic promises	(Luke 1:13)	Zacharias and Elizabeth told they would have baby
Enlightens us	(Zechariah 1:9)	Daniel's heaven vision explained

Provide Heavenly resources	(1 Kings 19:5-8)	Angels fed Elijah in the wilderness when he fled from Jezebel
Partner with us	(Acts 8:26-40)	Directed Philip when ministering to an Ethiopian man
Communicate revelations	(Rev 1:1)	John's revelation
Rescues use	(Acts 7-10)	Recounting Joseph saving the people from famine
Bring healing from God	(John 5:4)	Angel stirred the waters of the healing pool of Bethesda
Strengthens us	(Luke 22:43)	Strengthened Jesus at Gethsemane
Fight for us	(Judges 6,7)	Gideon's battle with the Midianites won by the angels
Warns us	(Matthew 2:13)	Magi warned not to go back the same way they came
Instructs us	(Daniel 9:21-23)	Gabriel helped Daniel understand what to do about his vision
Assists in Relationships	(Genesis 24:7)	Angel helped find the bride for Issac
Surrounds us with protection	(Daniel 6:22)	Angels shut the mouths of the lions for Daniel
Explains God's ways	(Luke 1:34-38)	Explained to Mary what God was going to do through her
Encourage and comforts us	(Daniel 10:18-19, Acts 27:22-25)	Paul was encouraged that God would ensure His purposes after the shipwreck.

My Angel Stories

The story of my salvation and the love letter the Lord sent to me has been covered many times in this book series and is thoroughly shared in my *Clips that Move Mountains 2nd Edition* book. After three months of personal discipleship with Maureen, she mysteriously disappeared from my life. I had always wondered if she was an angel and five years ago, it was confirmed that she is my guardian angel! Here are some excerpts from *Clips that Move Mountains: 2nd Edition* that shares that story.

When I was in college, I had a boyfriend named Fred, whom I worshiped. He was a Christian, and I wasn't yet. But he was EVERYTHING to me. It was the tail end of freshman year and we had been together since the beginning of the year.

I was a member of a campus club that was having a planning retreat at a camp one weekend. Maureen was older than me and was assigned as my roommate for the weekend. We talked all night about God's love and his free gift of salvation. In the wee hours of the morning, I accepted Christ.

When I got back from that weekend, I was excited to share my decision with Fred. He had some news for me too. He told me that all weekend, he had gotten the sense that God wanted him to break up with me. He didn't know why but felt strongly that he needed to do it. I was devastated.

I immediately called Maureen and she told me that she was expecting my call. God had told her that Fred was going to break up with me and she had a letter for me. It was a letter from God about how He needed to be my first love. It was exactly what I needed. Maureen worked and prayed with me for several months teaching me from the Bible and helping me learn more about God.

Just when I was feeling better, I called Maureen on the same number that I had been calling her for months and a strange guy answered the phone. He said that they didn't know who Maureen was and that they had that number all year. I was confused. I searched for her contact information in the school registration office and could find no record of her. It seemed like she didn't exist. Had God used an angel to lead me to Him? I have always thought so. *Hebrews 13:2 says, "Don't forget to show hospitality to strangers, for some who have done this have entertained angels without realizing it!"* I never saw her again, but I look forward to seeing her in heaven someday and then I will know for sure.

I had that dog-eared letter for years and gave copies of it away to many people who had broken hearts and needed to know that God loved them. A part of me thought that Fred and I would get back together when we were both spiritually ready. But that wasn't God's plan.

George and I married 7 years later. As soon as I moved into our newlywed home, I lost that letter. It had been in my Bible all that time, and then suddenly, it was gone. I was heartbroken. It had become one of my treasured possessions. I had guessed that I lost it because God felt like I didn't need it anymore. But I have thought of it often. It had been lost to me for 25 years.

(The story of how the Lord returned the love letter and the letter itself is not included here. If you look up "believe it and be satisfied" on the internet, you will find that letter on multiple pages of the internet. For purposes of this story, that part of the story is not included here.)

The story picks up with how I discovered that Maureen is an angel.

I was working on a deliverance class called "Prayers the Heal the Heart" for my doctorate. I had some work to do to heal some heart wounds. I met Jesus in my Special Place in the spirit. He and I walked up the hill to the Sea of Galilee. Then, we lay on the ground and were looking and laughed at the clouds. Jesus thought that one looked like an elephant and I thought it looked like a duck. I was thinking about the people in the book (referencing the class book) that shared that God had healed them of memories by going back to the scene and allowing Him to reframe the circumstance and show them the truth they didn't see before.

You can ask Me to show you anything that you want to know.

Lord, as painful as it is to take me back to my heartbreak in 1979. Please show me where you were then as Maureen and I were talking and when you gave me the love letter.

Immediately, I was back in 1979, watching the scene as if like Scrooge, there but not really there.

I saw myself crying face down on my bed in my dorm room. I looked around and could see with great detail remembering what the room looked like. Then I saw Jesus lying next to me as I sobbed, and He was whispering in my ear. I walked over closer so I could hear what He was saying to me. He was speaking word for word the letter that I received in 1979. At that same moment, I saw the words being typed in the upper right corner of my mind's eye. As Jesus spoke the words, they were appearing on the paper in heaven. Then I saw Jesus giving the paper to Maureen.

Then the Lord gave me short vignette glimpses of Maureen and me as she gave me the letter, and of us studying the Word together.

Then I saw myself trying to call her and Jesus was standing next to me when I was talking to the guys who answered the phone. I was confused as they said they had that number all school year. As I heard myself talking to the guys on the phone, Jesus was whispering in my ear... *"You don't need her anymore... you have Me now..."* He was repeating that in my ear as I hung up the phone in lost confusion.

Wow, Lord. That really helps me understand this situation so much more. You were with me the entire time! Please show me Maureen now so I can thank her for what she did for me.

Suddenly, we were back at my special place still lying on the grass and we sat up on the hill. Jesus pointed toward the Sea and I saw Maureen walking up the hill to greet us. She was dressed in a Roman dress with a breastplate of armor and had long dark and flowing hair. She looked a bit like I remember her, but she didn't have glasses, and she still looked young. She hugged me and I hugged her and could feel her wings... soft, strong, and powerful. She had a meekness about her; strength under control.

Then the Lord gave me short images of Maureen with me as a child sitting on my bed as I was crying because I could hear my parents fighting. I saw another where she was sitting and laughing as my young sibs and I were hanging our feet off the back of our powder blue station wagon. And I saw her with Jesus when He gave her the letter and the assignment to share it with me.

Just like Me, she has been with you all along. She is your Guardian Angel.

I thanked them both and cried... it was an overwhelming vision! Maureen and I have had many adventures together since then. Not the least of which was experiencing what the shepherds saw on the night of Jesus' birth. Ask, seek, and knock and you can have Jesus adventures like this too!

There are many more stories that I could share, but one was a result of one of the encounters at the end of this chapter. I asked the Lord to show me a time that angels helped me out when I was unaware.

When my oldest daughter, Jamael, was in middle school. Her sisters attended another school. Because the schools were not far from each other, but farther from home, I would pick up Jamael and she would wait with me until it was time to pick up her sisters.

On this day, she said she had too much homework and asked me to take her home first. She typically sat in the front passenger seat of my car. I was driving northbound to pick up the girls and a deer jumped out from behind a development sign and was struck by a southbound car. In slow motion, I saw this deer fly into the air, flip a full tuck and crash through my windshield. It slammed against my front passenger seat and flew back out the window, bouncing on the hood before landing on the ground in front of my car.

I was covered in broken glass, but completely unhurt. A man was mowing his yard across the street and rushed to see if I was OK. He called the police and invited me into his home to wait for the police. I remember telling him how shaken up I was that Jamael could have been killed if she was with me that day!

Twelve years later that man became my daughter's father-in-law! It would be about six years before my daughter and his son, Nick would date and another six years before they got married. They have our three beautiful grandchildren. God used the angels to protect the futures and destinies of an entire family that day!

Your Authority Related to Angels

Christ began higher than the angels as part of the Godhead, then for a little while became man. Mankind was created lower than angels and when Jesus took on human form, He was 100% man.

> Hebrews 2:9 But we do see Jesus, who was made lower than the angels for a little while [by taking on the limitations of humanity], crowned with glory and honor because of His suffering of death so that by the grace of God [extended to sinners] He might experience death for [the sins of] everyone.

Jesus was restored to His former glorified self when He was resurrected. All are subject to the authority of Christ. Our union with

186

Christ positions us as co-heirs with Christ raising us higher than angels. Exercising the power and authority we have in this union is part of our great inheritance.

Ephesians 1:18-20 (The Passion Translation) [18] I pray that the light of God will illuminate the eyes of your imagination,[a] flooding you with light, until you experience the full revelation of the hope of his calling[b]—that is, the wealth of God's glorious inheritances that he finds in us, his holy ones!

[19] I pray that you will continually experience the immeasurable greatness of God's power made available to you through faith. Then your lives will be an advertisement of this immense power as it works through you! This is the mighty power [20] that was released when God raised Christ from the dead and exalted him[c] to the place of highest honor and supreme authority[d] in the heavenly realm! [21] And now he is exalted as first above every ruler, authority, government, and realm of power in existence! He is gloriously enthroned over every name that is ever praised,[e] not only in this age,[f] but in the age that is coming![g]

[22] And he alone is the leader and source of everything needed in the church. God has put everything beneath the authority of Jesus Christ[h] *and has given him the highest rank above all others.*

I asked Jesus to help us understand our authority and how we can cooperate with the ministry of angels.

Angels are an extension of Me and they exercise My will. In that way, they are just like you when you obey My voice and minister to others. I like working through others!

I am always with you and your angels are always with you. When you are daydreaming while driving, for example, and then suddenly you are aware that you need to break for a traffic light, you can thank the angel that got your attention.

Remember when you were at the Jesus 18 conference and you saw the darting lights on the ceiling during the worship session? Those were my angels praising along with you. Angels are always around you. Always!

They are super fun! They are the most joyful of all My creations! This is because of their constant proximity to Me. Whatever you need, ask Me to involve angels and see what happens.

The more you are aware of the spiritual realm the more you will see and experience the blessings of angels. They are never to be worshipped. And they are not to be taken advantage of like personal genies. They are created to aid and fulfill My will for you. Never abuse the privilege of having them by your side. Honor them as a gift from Me to help you.

Angels love to be needed. Increase your sensitivity to the spirit realm and you will see them more. You have seen Maureen many times now that you have met her. Make sure you thank the angels when you are aware that they have helped you with something. Ask for an increase in that awareness as well.

Amen! Yes. Thank you, Lord!

Encountering the Lord of Hosts

Remember to meet the Lord as a child and allow Him to direct the encounters. Also, beginning each encounter with doing something fun with the Lord is always a great heart-posturing exercise.

1. Lord of Hosts, in what areas of my life do you want me to trust You to fight for me and protect me more? How specifically can I allow you to do that?

2. Lord of Hosts, please introduce me to my guardian angel(s). Allow me to have a conversation with my angel(s) so I can understand how they help me and thank them.

3. Lord of Hosts, show me specific times in my life when angels helped me and I was unaware.

4. Lord of Hosts, how can I cooperate more fully with the ministry of angels?

That's the Power by Hillsong Worship
https://youtu.be/oV1QHM72JTQ

The POWER Book Conclusion

$\mathcal{F}$or nearly every book conclusion I write, the Lord gives me a movie metaphor. It's just one of the creative ways that He communicates with me. Stephen Skelton receives messages from the Lord this way as well. His passion is to show people the biblical truths hidden in modern-day entertainment. He writes books and bible study's looking at the hidden biblical lessons in programming like the Andy Griffith Show, Bonanza, and even the Beverly Hillbillies.

What We Learn from Superman

In Skelton's book *The Gospel According to the World's Greatest Superhero,*[19] he shares the many parallels that Superman has with Jesus. The Superman character was conceived by two Jewish teenagers, Jerry Seigel, and Joel Shuster as a comic book in the 1930s. It was a dark time beginning with the rise and hellish impact of the Nazis, World War II, and the great depression. The world needed a hero, a savior.

---

[19] The Gospel According to the World's Greatest Supehero by Stephen Skelton, Harvest House Publishers, 2006

Whether intentional or unintentional, these young boys created a comic strip with a hero that reflected the nature and character of Jesus. Interestingly, the original name of Clark Kent's earthly parents were Mary and Joseph. Superman's given name was Kal-El from his home planet Krypton. Kal in the Hebrew lexicon means "to be completed or finished". El means God(s) or stands for the Trinity. It is the "isness" name of God that includes the fullness of all that God is, was, and ever will be. It is another name for Jehovah, I AM, and Yahweh. Krypton in Greek means "hidden". I think all of that is really interesting!

The boys were inspired by the Biblical characters of Samson as the strongest man alive, and Moses, the one who could lead people out of bondage and provide hope. "They were looking for a savior figure they could relate to, they could envision, something to give them hope, inspire them," Skelton said.

In this film clip from the Superman film from 1978, we see an 18-year-old (Kal-El) aka Clark Kent discovering his true identity and purpose while experiencing twelve years of mentorship and instruction from his biological father from his world of origin. He was thirty years old when he emerged as Superman. Interestingly, that was the same age Jesus began His earthly ministry.

Becoming Superman/Instructions from His Father
https://youtu.be/7ujuOikKgAE[20]

There are so many wonderful nuggets in this short clip. Here are some Jor-El quotes that remind me of some of what was covered in this book.

"Here in this fortress of solitude, we shall try to find the answers together." (Your special place to experience God personally.)

"You have great powers, only some of which you have yet discovered." (The manifestation gifts of the Holy Spirit within.)

"Come with me my son, as we break through the bounds of your earthly confinement." (Spend time abiding in Christ in the spiritual realm.)

"...pass through the flaming tunnel...you will enter the realm... source of your strength and nourishment." (Get fed and strengthened in the Word and by encounters with God)

"...examine the various concepts of immortality and its basis in actual fact". (Allow God to give you His eternal perspective, on earth as it is in heaven.)

"...total accumulation of all knowledge "...embedded in the crystals I have sent along with you. Study them well, my son. (The Word of God and its guidance when interpreted by the Holy Spirit.)

"Serve your world and its collective humanity" (Identify your destined purpose and live it out.)

"Live as one of them but discover where your strength and power will lead you" (You are in this world, but not of this world. Live set apart.)

---

[20] Brando and the Fortress of Solitude film clip from Superman (1978) https://youtu.be/7ujuOikKgAE. Posted by agoraphobicsuperstar.

"Always hold in your heart the pride of your special heritage." (Remember that you are a citizen of heaven with the rights and authority of the King of kings.)

"They can be a great people, Kal-El. They wish to be. They only lack the light to show them the way. For this reason, above all, their capacity for good, I have sent them you, my only son." (The Heavenly Father sent Jesus to make the way, then He sent the Holy Spirit to us, and we are called to reflect the light of God in this generation.)

This is not the first time the Lord brought Superman to my attention. When I was studying for my doctorate, I was pondering Romans 13:14 one day and asked the Lord to help me understand it.

> Romans 13:14 But clothe yourselves with the Lord Jesus Christ, and make no provision for [nor even think about gratifying] the flesh in regard to its improper desires.

> The Lord explained; *"I AM God Almighty. You can't borrow my might. You can't muster up strength without Me. All you*

can do is put on My strength like a garment. Allow ME to be your strength. Allow My strength to flow through your willing vessel."

"Consider Superman," the Lord continued, *"To the naked eye, Clark Kent was an average, awkward man. He drew no special attention when he walked down the street. He was like every other ordinary person on this planet. No one knew that he was a prince from an otherworldly kingdom or that he had superhuman powers. But, when those powers were needed, Clark stripped off his regular clothes to reveal that he was really covered with a superhero garment.*

There was a special place where Clark learned wisdom from his father and he spent much time there preparing for the responsibility of using his powers for doing good and combating evil. When Clark wore the clothes of his true nature, he displayed superhuman strength and abilities to the world. When evil was afoot, he knew exactly what to do. He performed miracles that blessed many people. Your superhero clothes are already there, underneath the surface. Let the world see them and I will do miraculous things through you!"

"Wow Lord, Believers in Christ are **exactly** like Clark Kent," I agreed.

This made me want to go to the Word and look for more evidence.

Ephesians 4:22-24 clarifies ..."[22]that, in reference to your former manner of life, you lay aside the old self, which is being corrupted in accordance with the lusts of deceit,[23]and that you be renewed in the spirit of your mind, [24]and put on the new self, which in the likeness of God has been created in righteousness and holiness of the truth...."

We are princes and princesses of the King of Kings and Lord of lords. We are to strip off the old garments of our former powerless selves to reveal the superior Godly ones like Clark does when he shows himself as Superman.

2 Peter 1:3-5 explains... "[3]seeing that His divine power has granted to us everything pertaining to life and godliness, through the true knowledge of Him who called us by His own glory and excellence. [4]For by these He has granted to us His precious and magnificent promises, so that by them you may become partakers of the divine nature, having escaped the corruption that is in the world by lust. [5]Now for this very reason also, applying all diligence, in your faith supply moral excellence, and in your moral excellence, knowledge..."

Because of the desire of the Father, the finished work of the Son, and through the power of the Holy Spirit, we **now** have the power and presence of God to do miraculous things according to God's will. To equip us, He shares with us His divine nature. With great power comes great responsibility. Like Clark, we need to spend time with our Father to truly understand and use this power appropriately.

The Lord added; *"You are ordinary and yet you have the capability of doing extraordinary things every day. You have My Word, prayer, and My presence to ensure that promise. Just like Clark, you need to discover who you are; the truth, assurances, and benefits of being My heir. My plans are bigger than what you can do alone and yet, I will always fully equip you to live them out. Your job is to discern My will and obey, the Lord said. Surrender your will to Mine and miracles will happen!"*

"How do we access that truth, Lord?" I asked.

"You need to find the answer to the question; who I really am? What are the promises of a child of the Living God? Spend time in My Word, listen to My voice, and be willing to do what I fully equip you to do according to My divine purposes. Believe the truth about who you are and allow it to transform you. Agree with the Me that I have the best plan for you and you will see a superhuman impact."

"So, the secret to the power is believing the truth of my identity in you. That's helpful Lord." I reflected.

If you are a believer in Christ, you **are** Superman/Superwoman. When a believer prays with a heart of faith, miracles happen. Just like Superman, these miracles often defy the physical laws of nature. Cancer simply disappears. Rain falls in the middle of a drought to stop a fire. Sight is restored to the blind. People are raised from the dead. People speak in unknown languages and souls are saved for eternity. God does miraculous things through those who surrender their will to the compassionate will of the Father.

Lord, Thank you that you are God Almighty. All might and strength come from You. Thank you that as a child of God, I can be clothed with your strength and righteousness and You can do miraculous things through me. Help me to desire to want Your will over my own and to not be afraid to let go of my plans in favor of Your miraculous ones. In Jesus' name, Amen.

Names You Met and Key Lessons

When you met the **Holy Spirit,** you gained a better understanding of His role as the third person of the Trinity. Salvation invites the Holy Spirit to dwell within the hearts of all new covenant believers. You learned the purpose of the Holy Spirit whose job it is to connect your spirit with God.

You took a deep dive into how to sense and cooperate with the Holy Spirit for your best Christian life. We learned all about the anointing and the manifestation gifts of the Holy Spirit brings when he comes in fullness in your heart.

We also discussed your role in cooperating with the Holy Spirit and releasing those gifts according to your testing purpose.

I asked Jesus what more He wanted you to take away related to the Holy Spirit, and this is what He said;

> *I cannot over-emphasize the importance of abiding in the Holy Spirit. The transformational power of allowing the Holy Spirit to mold you into the vessel I created you to become.*
>
> *Focus on me causes the anointing oil to be poured and smeared and rubbed on you in ways that cannot be missed. The more you boldly wear Me for all to see by the rubbing of the anointing oil poured on you because of abiding dries permanently like an indelible tattoo.*
>
> *People will "feel" Me when they are near you. They will be drawn to Me because of your boldness. Elisha's bones were so saturated by my presence that every atom in neuron remained on the prophet's bones because of his abiding in Me by the power of the Holy Spirit. It was a permanent imprint.*
>
> *Memory foam receives an imprint that pops back after you take your hands off of it. But when it happens over and over and over an imprint remains. Evidence of it remains visible after the person gets up. The same is true when the anointing is present repeatedly in your life because of abiding and allowing for the direction of the Holy Spirit in your life.*
>
> *Understanding how His power is your power within you is the key point of this Name.*

The un-deniable order and complexity of the fingerprint of God show powerful evidence of our **Creator**, Elohim. You learned how each of God's Omni-characteristics are revealed in God's creation.

We explored how the laws of the spirit realm are the same as the laws and quantum physics. Which helps us understand how the miraculous happens.

You also learn how God created you to be able to see her see and hear in the spirit according to the rules of the spirit. Understanding how the spiritual realm works increases your power to exercise your dual citizenship of heaven and earth.

This is what Jesus had to say about what he wants you to understand about the Creator.

> *You were created in Our image, and because all creation came from imagining and then speaking, you must understand the power of speaking in agreement with the words and pictures I give you.*
>
> *Guard your heart, mind, and mouth against anything that could limit your power and authority as a child of the living God.*
>
> *Understanding the incredible evidence that I AM your Creator by the majesty of creation and the power you have to create because you are In Me are the key lessons of this Name.*

We covered a lot of ground when we learned about **God Almighty**, El Shaddai, the Omnipotent ruler of all. We examined His nature and character, the things He does for us, and what He desires for and from us.

You discovered the seven things that are revealed in scripture that you can do to cooperate with His will and rule. We also did a deep dive into areas of your authority as a believer to battle offensively against the principalities of the evil spiritual realms. You learned specific strategies for releasing the power and authority by the power of Almighty God.

LORD, what do you have to say about your Name God Almighty?

> *I want you to realize the goodness of My Sovereignty and the power of your authority when surrendered to Me. I want you to fully understand what it means to partner with Me to usher in My perfect will and plan for all people. I want you to realize*

that I AM All Might, All Strength, All-Sufficiency. The key word here is ALL. There is no need I cannot meet and no enemy I cannot beat. In this world, there will be many challenges, needs, and trials. Through Me, you have the power to be victorious over all of them. In Me, you have all that you need.

The key lesson of this Name is to understand that MY job is to will and release the power and your job is to cooperate and allow Me to guide you. Partner with Me so together we can co-reign.

When you met the **God of Justice,** you learned that your salvation decision and the blood of Jesus break demonic contracts and free you from condemnation. You learned the importance of witnessing and testifying to the Truth as the powerful way to set you free. You learned that Jesus defends you and fights your battles when you allow Him to. Most of your battles are not even from this world, so learning the justice system of heaven helps you know how to ensure that you are not fighting against yourself. God IS the victory when you battle with Him.

What did the Lord want you to learn from this name:

I want you to learn how to recognize when a battle is actually spiritual. Don't just look at natural circumstances. Call out My Name and ask Me to come and fight with you. Surrender every battle to Me because I NEVER lose. I ALWAYS win. I AM your Righteous King. It is a sweet aroma in My nostrils when you surrender and allow Me to be your Defender.

When you met the **Lord of Hosts** you learned that your dual citizenship enables you to connect with and cooperate with angels in the spiritual realm. There is an entire spiritual realm surrounding you at all times and angels were created to help you get through life. Learning how to cooperate with the ministry of angels helps them help you. And they love to be helpful.

Lord, what did you most want people to take away about the Lord of Hosts?

As the Commander of the legions of angel armies, there is no army in any realm that is more powerful than My army. They are under MY command and obey my directions flawlessly. I cannot make a strategic mistake. Remember as a citizen of heaven and the son or daughter of the King of kings, you have the authority to ask for angel assistance so long as it is following My will. Remembering this will increase your own power and effectiveness in getting through your life challenges and serving Me. This little-known resource at your disposal is a mighty strategy for overcoming anything the enemy tries to through at you. Remember only one-third of the angels changed teams. They are outmatched, outwitted, outpowered, and outnumbered! Learn how to cooperate with My angels and watch what will happen!

Encounter Stories from Others

- **Sense ME- (Julie Sordi)**

Here is the song I was worshipping over and over when I saw in the heavenly realm. Hallelujah (Agnus Dei) by Amy Grant.

https://youtu.be/yDcJTp08114

Your senses; eyes, ears, breathing (nose), and heart. Worship (your throat and mouth). Your eyes focused on Me and Me only. Your voice worshipping Me and connected to your heart - wholeheartedness. Your breathing - being rested. Your ears listening to the music, listening to my voice. Asking, asking and continually asking. When it's your whole heart's desire. The closer you get to Me the more you will see... but, don't forget to ask Me to see it. The more you live in your purpose with Me the more you will see!

- **Angel Guidance (Pastor George Medellin)**

As I was praying in the Spirit, I saw in the Spirit a large fire person waving to me from my hallway (I was in the living room sitting). I tested the spirit and it claimed to serve the Lord Jesus Christ of Nazareth who came in the flesh. I then asked, "What would you like to say?" The response, "Cooperate with me and you'll see things you never dreamed of - of course, we'll point all to the Lord Jesus Christ of Nazareth who came in the flesh. He loves you so much."

At 4:47 a.m., the fire person (who I believe is/was an angel of revival) waves to me again from the hallway and invites me to come over. As I walked over, I felt prompted to kneel and the fire angel put a crown of fire on my head. *"This is so you can usher in the revival that's been talked about. Do it. Do all that He's put in your heart."* I believe Holy Spirit then said this to me, *"Yes, son. I've equipped you with the authority to advance My interests. Do as I say. You'll see things you never thought imaginable."*

- **I Hear you, Holy Spirit (Cindy Fiebig)**

Lord, increase my sensitivity to your voice. Give me specific tips and tools that will help me hear you more easily and not doubt your voice.

> *Listen! I AM always here, you only need to pause and listen. If you will stop with each breath and ask Me to speak, you will hear Me. I will show you what I have for you to do.*

> *My voice is in your heart. Sometimes it sounds like your conscience. Sometimes it sounds like your own thoughts. You have heard that I speak between your thoughts. What if, when you are having a conversation with yourself, you're really talking to Me? Listen more intently to those back and forths. You can discern when it is Me speaking – you know enough of My Word to discern My voice. If you are unsure, just ask. I will confirm My voice with you.*

I want you to hear Me with each thought. Yes, that is possible, just ask.

A thought comes, Lord, where are you?

I AM here.

What are you doing?

I am speaking. I am showing you something I want you to see. Acknowledge what you hear and what you see and act when I give you direction to act. If you will form the habit of asking me with each thought, I will be able to do great things through you. The time is coming to begin developing the discipline to live out of My will and your heart.

- **My Trips to the Courts of Heaven (Dianne Wright)**

The Word says to "enter His gates with thanksgiving and His courts with praise" Two of my heavenly court experiences stand out in my mind.

Once I went to the court to pray about generational curses. Some curses we are whereof and many we are not but we can bring them all there in the spirit of humility. Because of our imperfections and the mistakes that we can make and agree with the devil has every right to accuse us. But because of the blood of Jesus I can cover myself with Jesus's humility confess and repent and ask for can forgiveness.

In the court, I saw many long lines of people and I saw things scales leaves and branches fall off of them for as far as I could see. I didn't understand why there were so many lines. Later I learned that it's not just about my immediate parents or grandparents but their spouses' lines and former spouses' and stepchildren's lines and grandchildren's lines. That's a lot of people! But the blood can cover it all!

The second time I was at the court I remember the Lord telling me to bring a weapon. I was expecting something like a sword or a shield, but the Lord had me bring a pen. My weapon is my testimony! After that experience, the Lord gave me the assignment to write a book!

I also wanted to mention that every time I go to the court of heaven, I do not go as an adult. I always see myself as a child bursting through the doors to see "my Daddy". I believe childlike faith is important when approaching the courts of heaven.

- **The Creator Speaking Through a Rainbow (Jesse Sliter)**

At a pre-prayer service before church, Jesse shared that while driving over the weekend he saw the beginning and the end of a rainbow. The center was wrapped in black clouds obscuring his view of it.

While pondering the rainbow he heard the Lord speak in his spirit reminding him that the symbol of the rainbow in the Bible is about God's promise keeping nature. God reminded Jesse to keep his eyes fixed on the promises He has given him about his ministry and life. Even though he can't see how God is moving him forward toward those promises, like the clouds that are obstructing his view of the rainbow, God is still moving him toward those promises. Only in hindsight will he realize that. But for now, thank and praise God for the things He is doing behind the scenes and live faithfully one day at a time.

Appendix A
Dialogue Journaling Tips

*T*his is a handy resource guide for you as you are learning how to incorporate dialogue journaling into your everyday spiritual life.

Know which voice you are hearing

- **God's Voice– spontaneous positive** thoughts, pictures, and feelings consistent with any Name of God, Character of God, or Nature of God. (Any of the Fruit of the Spirit, "Omni" truths, and compound Names of God). God can speak through images, stories, emotions, music, and sparks of creative insight... God speaks the language of the heart.

- **Satan's voice– spontaneous negative** thoughts, pictures, and feelings consistent with his character and nature. (Lying, deceiving, tears down, lead you away from faith in God). Listening to this voice will lead to faith in reverse and will amplify worry.

- **Your own thoughts – analytical, practical, logical.** Your thoughts speak in the language of the head. They may even look like a list of practical concerns, but remember, the LORD offers solutions.

Don't expect it to look or sound a certain way. God's ways are different from your ways. Your specific expectations can be a significant barrier to hearing from God. He does not need to sound like a booming voice.

Give God credit for when He speaks to you or shows you something spontaneously. That brilliant idea that came to you in the meeting, for example, was God. Make sure you thank Him for it. Likewise, **don't take credit for negative thoughts** or pictures that are self-deprecating or send you backward in your faith. Those thoughts are from the enemy and the sooner you recognize them and rebuke the enemy out loud, the faster they will cease. Rebuking out loud is important because the enemy is not Omniscient. He doesn't know your thoughts. So, speak with the authority of God when you recognize these negative messages.

Have **spiritual counselors** to help you make sure you are hearing from God. The characteristics of a good spiritual counselor are:

- They should **know the Word, have a close relationship with God, and be able to discern His Voice themselves. They should also be humble enough to have spiritual advisors themselves.**

- **Submit your journaling** to a counselor when **you are learning** how to discern God's voice.

- **Submit your journaling** to a counselor to **people with more experience** in an area where you have specific issues for which the LORD is addressing.

206

- **Submit your journaling** to a counselor when you get a message **that does not seem consistent with God's Character.** Remember, God's Voice will be full of faith, hope, and love. He will gently and lovingly convict of sin but will not condemn or tear you down.

- **Submit your journaling** to a counselor if it is related to a **major life transition, or if you feel that what you received doesn't feel or sound like God.**

Don't try – Striving to hear from God is you trying in your own effort. This does not work, and you will likely get a journal that analyzes your circumstances logically. This is not from God. You need to relax **and let God take the wheel.** It's much easier than you might expect.

Imagine yourself as a small child. This connects you with your inner child and **awakens childlike faith.**

It doesn't have to be perfect. Don't put off talking to God because you want everything to be perfect and you want to have a lot of time to do it. **It doesn't require a lot of time** to speak to Jesus. A few minutes of quality time with Jesus is much better than not spending time with Him at all.

Avoid evaluating what you are receiving from the LORD as you are getting it. **Evaluation at the moment is doubt.** When you begin to doubt the validity of the experience, you hang up on Jesus. Allow yourself to receive the flow of the Holy Spirit freely, knowing you can evaluate it later.

Evaluate what you have received after your time with Jesus is complete. The message should be consistent with Scripture and the

Names and Character of God. God is all about faith, hope, and love. Even if the Lord is giving you constructive discipline, your message from the LORD should build you up, help you feel loved, and give you hope. If it doesn't, then it's worth passing by a spiritual counselor.

How to avoid distractions

Internal distractions like having a lot of things on your mind can be dealt with by pulling out paper and **writing a list of the things that you need to do** so you won't forget them. That way you can set them aside and focus on the LORD.

External distractions – Find a place where you know that no one will bother you. If necessary, use noise-canceling earphones or relaxation music with no crescendos. And, no one bothers you in the bathtub. ;-)

Ways to quiet yourself down

Deep breathing- Breathe in the Power of the Holy Spirit, exhale anxiety and other negative thoughts. It's relaxing and helps you focus on Jesus.

Find a **comfortable place and position**- Don't get so comfortable that you fall asleep. Although, God certainly can and does speak to us in dreams! Comfortable means that you are not distracted by pain but are not so relaxed that you fall asleep.

If **music** is helpful, that's great. Just make sure that it is **instrumental and has a steady rhythm**. You don't want the music to lead the experience. That's Jesus' job. The songs in this book are more for worship and meditation which posture your heart for connecting with God. For quiet meditation, however, go with relaxing instrumental songs. I find that "Classic Music for Studying" and "Instrumental Christian" are great Pandora[21] stations for journaling.

Singing or praying in tongues is a wonderful way to get your eyes on Jesus. When you have surrendered your mouth, you can know that the Holy Spirit is fully engaged, and your heart is made ready for Jesus. It is a guaranteed way to make sure that Jesus is taking the wheel. However, if this is not a gift that God has released in you yet, do *not* stress about it or feel that God is not speaking to you. Ask God to open the door for the gift of tongues to be released in you. He will answer that prayer.

Capturing the flow of the Holy Spirit

Always begin by **fixing your eyes on Jesus**. It's OK if you don't see Jesus' face or whole body at first. That is common. But don't let that make you think it's not real or isn't working. Sometimes people can just feel His loving Presence and that's enough. The point is that **He needs to be your focus.**

Speak with and experience only the One True God. Don't pray to your deceased relatives or any other entities. You are speaking to the Father through Jesus, by the power of the Holy Spirit. You can call directly to any Names of the Godhead (Jesus, Heavenly Father, Holy Spirit, or any of God's Names), just don't pray to or worship anyone else.

I encourage you to set the stage for your conversation with Jesus by meeting with Him in **your special place**, for example. But once He is in the scene, **take your hands off the wheel and let Him take**

---

[21] www.Pandora.com

over. The purpose of the special place is to give you an anchoring place to collect memories of Jesus that make it easier to trust that you can see Him again there whenever you need to. You don't need to always see Him there, however. And, God can change your special place over time.

Some people can and like to **write down the conversation** as it is happening. I do this. It's just capturing what the LORD is saying as He is saying it. This is especially important if you are using the ears of your heart to hear Him speak. **Others need to see the scene without pulling out the paper and writing.** When I ask God for a visual experience, I do this. If this is you, then make sure to ask the LORD to help you remember everything important so you can write it down afterward. I want to keep looking and the LORD is faithful to help me remember every detail that I experienced. When the vision is complete, I journal what I saw.

Writing your journal conversations and experiences is important, even if you don't like writing. Your journal provides a **written record** of what the LORD has said and shown you. It is also a log **of your answered prayers**. I always re-read my journals when they are full and it's amazing to remember the experiences I had with Jesus that I may have forgotten.

Remember that this is **a conversation with God**, keep looking, keep talking, and **ask follow-up questions** like you would if you were talking to a friend. Write down the flow of that conversation.

A **song** rolling around in your head can be a message from God. I like to look up the lyrics of a song that is stuck in my head. There is nearly always a message in the lyrics that is exactly what I needed that day.

What to do when you are stuck

Watch how you talk about being stuck. Don't activate faith in reverse by saying out loud that "I can't do this." You can do it; you just need to believe that you can do it because the LORD promises that everyone can do it. **Speak in agreement with what God says.**

Confess and repent of any unbelief and ask God to increase your faith so that you can relax and be able to hear and see Him.

Ask the LORD if there is any unconfessed sin that may be blocking your ability to hear. **Confess and repent of that sin** and try it again.

If you are still stuck, fast and **pray for the LORD to show you** the specific block. You may have a feeling, a person's name pop into your mind, or a conflict that needs to be addressed. Listen and do what He says to get the flow back.

Things to avoid

God is not a genie or a magic 8 ball. For this reason, **avoid asking predictive questions** about your future. The LORD will reveal promises and glimpses of your future when and if He desires. Trust Him one day at a time. Ask Him about today. Matthew 6:11 says; "Give us this day."

Along the same lines, **avoid telling Jesus how you want things to go,** or what you think should happen. This is a learning curve for sure, but things will go much better for you when you learn to let God take control. Keep your attitude humble and faithful.

Great Questions to Ask Jesus

It is helpful to focus your prayer by **calling on the Name of God** that is related to your issue: Some examples are:

211

- Jehovah Jireh, how can I cooperate with your provision?

- Good Shepherd, what do you want me to do today?

- Comforter, you know every heart and every motivation, show me their heart. Or, Show me my heart.

- Great I AM, You are the Source of all wisdom, please give me wisdom in this circumstance.

- Mighty Counselor, You know the very best course of action for this circumstance; what do you want me to say or do in this situation today?

- LORD, you are the Author of my story, what is the step I can take today to move forward toward the promise you have given me?

- Great Physician, what do I need to do to receive your healing? What is the condition that I need to meet to receive healing?

- Word of God, help me understand these Scripture verses. No one can explain them better than He can.

- Ask Jesus about Biblical concepts like abiding in Him, forgiveness, surrender, Old Testament concepts and their New Testament parallels, the Trinity, creation, etc. Anything you want to understand more about your faith, the Bible, and your relationship with Him is OK to ask. He is not too busy to answer these questions. God delights in answering them.

Pour your heart out to God. You can be brutally honest with God. He knows everything anyway. There's no point in trying to be phony with God. Your best friend wouldn't put up with that, so why should Jesus? After you vent, make sure you pause and listen. This is what made King David the man after God's own heart.

Remember to **let Jesus do most of the talking**. If your journals are filled with your venting and no responses from Jesus, you are missing a huge blessing. This is "dialogue journaling", not "monologue journaling." Dialogue journaling is your prayers with God's response in conversations and experiences. What He has to say is the more important part of the conversation. Also, when the Lord pours His heart out to you, thank Him. **Reply to Him that you understand what He is saying and the purpose in your spirit to obey Him.**

Adventures to have with Jesus

- **Enter a Bible scene-** If you have read about an experience that someone had in the Bible, you can ask Jesus to give you this experience. A few nice ones that I have had the pleasure of experiencing were talking with Jesus at the well, walking on water, listening to Jesus give the Sermon on the Mount, and watching David write a psalm. The Bible is full of wonderful stories and Jesus loves to take us on adventures.

- **A shared Bible story experience-** The above idea can also be experienced as a group. My Bible study group experienced the Day of Pentecost by meditating together on Acts 1:1-21. The LORD showed each of us something different and we shared what we saw as we were prompted by Him to do so. Our experiences rounded out a beautiful picture together!

- **Jesus will often take you on adventures** without you asking for them. If He wants you to understand something, He will take you to a place and allow you to experience an activity that will send the exact message that He has for you. **Be willing to follow Him on that adventure.**

213

- A great healing opportunity is to **ask Jesus to take you to a difficult time in your past** and ask Him to show you either where He was at the time or give you His perspective on it. Just seeing Him there can be all it takes to lead you to forgiveness.

- **Ask the LORD to give you a picture, story, metaphor, or parable** that will help you understand a Biblical concept or a complicated situation you are facing. This is exactly how Jesus taught people while He was on Earth. So, we know that He loves to do that and will do that for you as you work through the encounter exercises in this book. He speaks in your personal language and brings in elements from your own life to help you understand things.

How to Call on the Names and Promises of God

The easiest way to find anything in the Bible is to simply put the search term in any computer browser. If you want scripture about healing, simply put 'verses about healing' for example. I guarantee many people have already written blogs or created lists on this topic for you! If you want to find a Bible story, simply type a search word or phrase such as 'verses walking on water 'and the verses about Peter's experience will pop up.

For a more in-depth Biblical study, BibleGateway.com has an advanced search capacity. In addition to just putting in a keyword, verse, or topic in the main search bar, there is a "keyword search" just below that bar that allows you to search 3 ways: **match all words, match any word, match exact phrase.** I will indicate below which of those matching keywords I used to come up with the recommended lists accordingly. Play around with this capability. The more specific you are in your keyword search, the more results that match what you are actually looking for will come up.

You may also play around with parallel scriptures or do these search terms with different Bible versions. The app and website have wonderful flexibility.

Finding the Name of God in Scripture:

Perhaps the best overall search for the Names of God is to **search "God is"** (exact phrase). This will give you 1376 verses in the NIV and is a wonderful way to learn in much more detail about the "Is-ness" of God.

- Example: 1 John 4:16 "And so we know and rely on the love God has for us. **God is love**. Whoever lives in love lives in God, and God in them."

Along those lines, the search **"I am"** will return 967 verses in the NIV (exact word order search).

- Example: Genesis 17:1 "When Abram was ninety-nine years old, the LORD appeared to him and said, "**I am God Almighty**; walk before me faithfully and be blameless.""

Look for the intention of the Scripture. The verse doesn't need to include the Name of God in it to address the topics or areas of concern under the Name's jurisdiction. **Ask, "What is the key action of this Scripture?"**

- Example: Jeremiah 30:17 "For I will restore you to health And I will heal you of your wounds,' declares the LORD..." The key action of this verse is to restore health and heal wounds. The Great Physician is the Name of God in this verse.

To look for the Name of God, I **look at the key action or character** represented in the verse. Is the verse trying to give me comfort? Then the Name of God may be the Comforter. Is the verse giving me wisdom or advice? Then it's probably the Mighty Counselor that is speaking. Is God fighting for me in this verse? Then it may be addressing the Shield, the Banner, or the Mighty Warrior. Is the verse suggesting leading us in a certain direction or giving us guidance in our lives? Perhaps it is referencing the Good Shepherd or the Author. If it's about physical, emotional, mental, or physical needs, then it could be addressing the Great Physician and Healer.

Finding the Promises of God:

To look for a promise in the Bible **look for absolute words** such as 'will', 'always', 'forever', or 'never', as opposed to 'sometimes', and 'might' kinds of statements. There are a lot of absolute words in the Bible if you look for them.

- Example: Deuteronomy 31:6 Be strong and courageous. Do not be afraid or terrified because of them, for the LORD your God goes with you; he **will never leave you nor forsake you**." The promise here is that the LORD will never leave or forsake you!

Searching (all words search) **'promises, God'**. 80 verses will pop up for you in the NIV. Or (all words search) **'covenant, God'** and 81 verses will pop up for that one.

- Example: Psalm 85:8 "I will listen to what **God the** LORD **says**; He **promises** peace to His people, His faithful servants— but let them not turn to folly."

Finding the Conditions of the Promise:

When looking for conditions of a promise, search for words like **"if,"** **"when," and "then"** kinds of words.

- Example: 2 Chronicles 7:14 "**If** my people, who are called by my Name, will humble themselves and pray and seek my face and turn from their wicked ways, **then** I will hear from heaven, and I will forgive their sin and will heal their land." Humility, seeking God's face, and turning from wicked ways are the conditions required for the promise of healing their land.

"**Therefore**" is a word that tells me that I need to look for the **context of a promise** or a command. Whenever you see the word, "therefore," ask God, what is that "there for"? Look at one or two verses before to find the context when the word "therefore" is present.

- Example: Matthew 19:67 "So they are no longer two, but one flesh. What **therefore** God has joined together, let no man separate." The unity of the two becoming one flesh is the context for the command for no man to separate them.

Noticing when the conditions are commands.

A **command is directive language**. You can tell a directive when it begins the sentence and directives are usually commanding verbs. It is intentional and strong.

- Example: Matthew 7:7 "**Ask**, and it **will** be given to you; **seek**, and you **will** find; **knock**, and it **will** be opened to you...." Ask, seek, and knock are the directives. The three uses of "will" show you to the promises.

Notice that the directives are also the conditions of the promise. You need to cooperate with the Holy Spirit in this verse to receive these promises.

How to pray with authority/without idols in your heart

- Before you pray, do some **Bible research** based on your issue and need. Using the tips above, find the Name, characteristic, or topic to research and find His promises categorically.

- **Call on the Name of God** relevant to your circumstance or issue.

- **Praise Him** for what that Name means for this situation.

- **Remind Him Who He is** and what He has promised.

- **Confess and repent** of any anxiety or unbelief that He can take care of in this situation.

- **Speak out loud that you agree with God**'s best plan and His sovereignty in this situation.

- **Ask Him to show you what the conditions** are for the healing or issue to be resolved.

- **Obey His instructions.**

- **Thank Him** for what you will learn and for how He will resolve this situation.

- **Praise Him** and end with "In Jesus' Name, Amen." This is important because you are claiming the authority of Jesus when you pray.

Practice this by taking any of the Names of God in this list and using the Scripture and promised identified, or what you have learned from researching the other search recommendations, write out a prayer that addresses your issue.

Example situation: You have just lost your job unexpectedly and have anxiety about the bills. You want peace in your heart. An example prayer is below the Name listing:

Prince of Peace

Found in: Philippians 4:6-7 [6]"Do not be anxious about anything, but in every situation, by prayer and petition, with thanksgiving, present your requests to God. [7] And the peace of God, which transcends all understanding, will guard your hearts and your minds in Christ Jesus."

Promises made by this Name: Peace is part of the Fruit of the Spirit. We can't have it without God. The LORD wouldn't command us not to be anxious if it was impossible. He gives us the instructions in these verses. Surrender all to Him and He will give you peace!

Other Verses or Search Terms

- Isaiah 9:6

- Ephesians 2:11-18

- John 14:27

- John 16:33

- Galatians 5:22

- Peace, God- 42 verses

- Peace, Spirit- 9 verses

- Peace, Jesus- 27 verses

Your Turn Practice Exercises:

Example Prayer: LORD, you are my Prince of Peace. You know that I have lost my job, and You have commanded me not to be anxious. You promise me that You will give me peace in all situations. I thank You for this turn of events because I trust that you are guarding my heart against fear and will bless me with Your Peace in this circumstance. I surrender this situation to You and trust You to guide me in Your Peace. What do You want me to know or to do today to receive Your Peace in this situation? Let the peace that transcends all understanding wash over me. I thank You and praise You, In Jesus' Name, Amen.

1. Practice praying this same situation over using another Name from the list. Perhaps the Author, Shepherd, or Provider would be a good start.

2. Now choose an issue that is relevant to you, choose a Name from the chart, and practice this prayer on your own issue.

3. How do you feel now that you prayed this way?

Bible Resources Online

- YouVersion is a resource that will help you stay in the Word. It's a Bible app you can download from any app store for your mobile devices and by www.youversion.com on your computer. You can **read, listen to and watch videos of the Bible in more versions than you even knew existed**. Bible reading plans help me **read the Bible every day**. Other app capabilities include parallel versions, notes, creating verse images, and posting Bible verses on social media.

- BibleGateway is an app and great website resource for Scripture searches. It has **advanced search capabilities** that allow you to filter your search by offering a variety of specific filters such as languages, topics, match categories (such as exact phrase, all words, or any word), and side-by-side parallel versions. Download It from your app store or visit www. Biblegateway.com.

- Biblehub is for the serious Bible researcher. Just about every Bible study resource can be found on this app and website. Once you type a verse on the home search screen you find on that same results page, the Scripture in context (one verse before and one after), **parallel versions, cross-references, and commentaries**. There are simply too many features of this app to mention, but this one is great when you want to dive into the Word and **research from many different angles.** Check out www.Biblehub.com.

- The Web Bible Encyclopedia by ChristianAnswers.net has a dictionary of **939 Names and Titles of God** with links to Scriptures that reference them. They are also distinguished by Hebrew, Greek, Aramaic, and Latin. You can use the Bible research tools below to dive into any of them on this site. http://www.christiananswers.net/dictionary/namesofgod.html

Appendix B
Salvation Prayer

⌒𝒮𝒮⌒

cts 10:36 reminds us that Jesus is LORD of all. That means that He is LORD of everyone, not only those who accept His gift of salvation and become children of God. It's another absolute truth of God. Some will realize that for the first time on Judgement Day when we will all experience Romans 14:11 "As surely as I live, says the LORD, every knee will bend to Me, and every tongue will confess and give praise to God." So then, each of us will give an account of ourselves to God.

Still, for those that choose to accept the gift of salvation, we have the right to become children of God.

> John 1:12 (NIV) Yet to all who did receive him, to those who believed in his Name, he gave the right to become children of God.

We have the power to share in God's divine nature and character and truly live the lives that He has planned for us from the beginning of time.

Jeremiah 29:11-14 (NIV) [11]For I know the plans I have for you," declares the LORD, "plans to prosper you and not to harm you, plans to give you hope and a future. [12]Then you will call on me and come and pray to me, and I will listen to you. [13]You will seek me and find me when you seek me with all your heart. [14]I will be found by you," declares the LORD, "and will bring you back from captivity."

If you haven't accepted Christ's gift of salvation and you are ready to do that, it's really simple. Just have a conversation with Jesus, and He will hear your heart cry. Admit that you need Jesus. Ask God for forgiveness. Believe that Jesus came to save you. Accept the free gift. Confess with your mouth that you receive the gift. Thank Him for saving you. There are no magic words to make that happen. He will accept your heartfelt prayer and send the Holy Spirit to dwell in your heart. It's that simple.

It could go something like this: Jesus, I'm tired of living my life without you. Forgive me for all my sins and for trying to do this life on my own without You. I need You to come and help me. I believe that You are who You say You are, Jesus. Thank you for offering me the way to eternal life. Come into my life now and show me how to be my best self, LORD. Thank you for sending me the Holy Spirit to show me the Way.

Once you have sincerely prayed a prayer like this, you are saved. Congratulations and welcome to the family!

Appendix C
How to Teach People to Journal

*I*f learning how to journal has changed your relationship with God and your life, and you want others to know how simple it is, please follow these simple steps so you can teach people how to connect with God as you can. This process can take only 30 minutes; with 15 minutes to explain it, and 15 minutes to experience God and discuss it.

1. **Induce Hunger-*Why should people want to know how to hear God's voice personally?***

   a. MOST IMPORTANTLY- Share your own story of how using this tool has changed your relationship with the Lord and changed your life. If you have a journal example you would like to share, that is usually what makes people want to try it!

   b. Ask them; Would you like to have the God who created heaven and earth speak to you by name about issues in your life; show you how to solve your problems, explain the Bible to you, give you direction, and personally heal you?

c. Explain that the Names of God are personal, such as the Bridegroom, Mighty Counselor, Friend, Defender, Provider, and Healer. Would you marry, seek counseling, trust your secrets, and lean on when you were in crisis, someone you can't see, hear or feel? God has these Names because He showed up as these Names to people in the Bible and they personally encountered Him in these ways. So can you.

2. Normalize it- *Hearing from God is normal and easy.*

a. God created everyone to see and hear Him with the eyes and ears of their heart. If you were unable to do so, you would never have accepted Him as your Savior in the first place. God is not willing for ANY to perish, so He wired us to be able to communicate with Him.

b. The entire Bible was written using the same four keys I will teach you in a few minutes.

c. Two-thirds of the Bible came to people who heard from God and they wrote it down and one-third of the Bible came when people received messages from the Lord by dreams and visions and they wrote it down. In all cases, they were using the ears and eyes of their hearts to connect with God.

d. God is the same yesterday, today, and forever (Hebrews 13:8). So, if this is how He spoke to Bible writers, He can do it now too. Even more so now that we have the Holy Spirit whose job is to endue us with the power to connect with God's nature and release His love to others. This direct access to Father God is what Jesus accomplished for us on the cross.

3. Address New Age Concern upfront- *It is different than what the New Agers do...*

a. When you ask for Jesus, you get Jesus. Matthew 7:9-11 New American Standard Bible (NASB) [9] Or what man is there among you [a]who, when his son asks for a loaf, [b]will give him a stone? [10] Or [c]if he asks for a fish, he will not give him a snake, will he? [11] If you then, being evil, know how to give good gifts to your children, how much more will your Father who is in heaven give what is good to those who ask Him?

b. New Agers seek a generalized spiritual realm and they get negative spirits.

c. We **can** know which voice-

   i. God sounds like His Names and character (fruit of the Spirit, build you up, encourage and edify, disciplines lovingly but does not condemn).

   ii. The enemy sounds like his names and character (lies, deceit, tears down, robs, steals, destroys, condemns). Condemnation speaks in generalities and results in guilt, shame, and negative identity whereas conviction is specific loving feedback and leads to repentance, healing, and restoration.

   iii. Your voice is logical and analytical and is limited to a natural world understanding.

4. **Share the Four Keys to Hearing God's Voice-** *There are four simple steps to hearing God's voice.*

a. **Quiet yourself down-** Externally and internally

b. **Fix your Eyes on Jesus**... ask and expect to see, hear, and feel from Him

c. **Tune to spontaneity-** allow the pictures, thoughts, and feelings to bubble up... don't try too hard

d. **Write down what you saw, heard, and felt,**

These steps can be seen in action in Habakkuk 2:1-2

Verse segment	How it relates to the 4 Keys
[1]I will stand on my guard post And station myself on the rampart;	He found a quiet place so he could look up to God. He was posturing his heart to speak to God Himself.
And I will keep watch to see what He will speak to me,	He was looking and listening with an expectation to hear from God personally... using the eyes and ears of his heart.
And how I may reply when I am reproved.	Habakkuk knew it would be a conversation with God. He knew that he could be able to hear what God had to say AND that he could reply.
[2]Then the LORD answered me and said,	God did reply personally.
"Record the vision and inscribe *it* on tablets, That the one who reads it may run.	God commanded Habakkuk to write down what He was going to say... writing it down is not just for you to be able to remember, but it can also be a blessing for others.

5. **Preparing for your first Jesus Encounter-**

a. Manage expectations--- God's voice sounds like your own thoughts and pictures on the screen of your mind but spontaneously and with His character... it's a bit more loving than you are usually.

b.   Practice seeing with the eyes of your heart. Close your eyes and picture your kitchen or bedroom of your house. Look around the room using the eyes of your heart. The clarity of the picture in your mind is the clarity of the image you will likely see when you go to see Jesus. So, it is not as clear as what you can see with your natural eyes, but you can still get an impression of what you are sensing.

c.   Practice hearing with the ears of your heart by closing your eyes and singing the Happy Birthday song in your mind.

d.   Some see easier and others hear easier, others get feelings. All of these are good beginnings. So, be happy with what you experience. All of us have these senses so, even if you are not experiencing all of them at first, you can ask God to give you increased sensitivity and practice. You will get better at it. So, don't despise small beginnings.

e.   Encourage them to imagine themselves as a child between the ages of 4 to 8 as this will help connect them to God with a more open heart because it activates their childlike faith.

6.   **The Special Place-** *Have a special place in your spirit where you can go and see Jesus there anytime.*

a.   This short, guided imagery will take you to a place of God's choosing for you to meet with Him. http://bit.ly/2g8v8iu

b.   How this guided imagery works, so you can facilitate something like it if you prefer.

i. Imagine a beautiful place. For some, it will be a place where they have been and where there are loving memories. For others, it is a beautiful place in general or even a supernatural place. The Lord knows exactly what place to pop into people's minds. Do not direct what this looks like. Relax and let the image pop into your mind. God speaks in your language, so even if it seems strange at first, go with it.

ii. Wake up and activate the Right-brain by asking them to see, hear, smell, and feel this place, left, front, right, up, and down. Speak it slowly enough for them to take in some details. This part is to make sure they are waking up their spiritual senses even before we introduce Jesus to the scene. Again, do not tell them what to see here, just tell them to look, and listen.

iii. Then ask them to turn around and see Jesus walking toward them. He has a smile on His face. When He approaches, He hugs them. This is specifically, so they see Jesus as His loving character.

iv. The first question that we recommend that they ask Jesus is "How do You feel about Me"? Then, completely take your hand off the wheel and let Jesus take it from there.

c. Give them time. Eight to ten minutes is usually a good amount of time. Then ask them to share their experience. If you are giving them the link above and they are not doing it now, schedule a time to review their first journal. This increases the likelihood that they do it.

d. Encourage them in their experience. This was a REAL Jesus encounter, not a figment of their imagination. Tell them that they can go back to the special place ANYTIME and Jesus will be there for them again.

Appendix D
Courts of Heaven Prayer Process
Case Example: You vs. Christ/You

*U*se this process example when you fix your eyes on your problems and not on Jesus leading to worry, anxiety, pride, fear, and negative outcomes.

Preparation for your Court of Heaven Encounter

Listen to and sing several worship songs to posture your heart to connect with Jesus. Praise and thank Him in advance for what He will do for you in this encounter.

Meditate on these scriptures... You can meditate by asking Lord in journaling to really help you understand any of these verses more before entering into the courtroom setting. Look for the words that tend to be highlighted for you and ponder and discuss them with Jesus. He would be happy to oblige! These are scripture examples chosen for this case purpose. You can ask the Lord to identify scriptures that apply to your area of concern or bondage.

Hebrews 4:16 [16] Therefore let us [with privilege] approach the throne of grace [that is, the throne of God's gracious favor] with confidence *and* without fear, so that we may receive mercy [for our failures] and find [His amazing] grace to help in time of need [an appropriate blessing, coming just at the right moment].

Hebrews 12:2 [2] [looking away from all that will distract us and] focusing our eyes on Jesus, who is the Author and Perfecter of faith [the first incentive for our belief and the One who brings our faith to maturity], who for the joy [of accomplishing the goal] set before Him endured the cross, [a]disregarding the shame, and sat down at the right hand of the throne of God [revealing His deity, His authority, and the completion of His work].

Romans 8:28-35 [28] And we know [with great confidence] that God [who is deeply concerned about us] causes all things to work together [as a plan] for good for those who love God, to those who are called according to His plan *and* purpose. [29] For those whom He foreknew [and loved and chose beforehand], He also predestined to be conformed to the image of His Son [and ultimately share in His complete sanctification], so that He would be the firstborn [the most beloved and honored] among many believers. [30] And those whom He predestined, He also called; and those whom He called, He also justified [declared free of the guilt of sin]; and those whom He justified, He also glorified [raising them to a heavenly dignity].

[31] What then shall we say to all these things? If God is for us, who can be [successful] against us? [32] He who did not spare [even] His own Son, but gave Him up for us all, how will He not also, along with Him, graciously give us all things? [33] Who will bring any charge against God's elect (His chosen ones)? It is God who justifies us [declaring us blameless and putting us in a right relationship with Himself]. [34] Who is the one who condemns us? Christ Jesus is the One who died [to

pay our penalty], and more *than that,* who was raised [from the dead], and who is at the right hand of God interceding [with the Father] for us. [35] Who shall ever separate us from the love of [a]Christ? Will tribulation, or distress, or persecution, or famine, or nakedness, or danger, or sword?

Joel 2:25-32

[25] "And I will compensate you for the years
That the swarming locust has eaten,
The creeping locust, the stripping locust, and the gnawing locust—
My great army which I sent among you.
[26] "You will have plenty to eat and be satisfied
And praise the name of the LORD your God
Who has dealt wondrously with you;
And My people shall never be put to shame.
[27] "And you shall know [without any doubt] that I am in the midst of Israel [to protect and bless you],
And that I am the LORD your God,
And there is no other;
My people will never be put to shame.

[28] "It shall come about after this
That I shall pour out My Spirit on all mankind;
And your sons and your daughters will prophesy,
Your old men will dream dreams,
Your young men will see visions.
[29] "Even on the male and female servants
I will pour out My Spirit in those days.

[30] "I will show signs *and* wonders [displaying My power] in the heavens and on the earth,
Blood and fire and columns of smoke.
[31] "The sun will be turned into darkness
And the moon into blood
Before the great and terrible day of the LORD comes.
[32] "And it shall come about that whoever calls on the name

of the LORD
Will be saved [from the coming judgment]
For on Mount Zion and in Jerusalem
There will be those who escape,
As the LORD has said,
Even among the remnant [of survivors] whom the LORD
calls.

Hebrews 12:24 [24] and to Jesus, the Mediator of a new covenant [uniting God and man], and to the sprinkled blood, which speaks [of mercy], a better *and* nobler *and* more gracious message than *the blood* of Abel [which cried out for vengeance].

Colossians 2:14 [14] having canceled out the [a]certificate of debt consisting of [b]legal demands [which were in force] against us and which were hostile to us. And this certificate He has set aside *and* completely removed by nailing it to the cross.

This is a case example. The underlined sections can be filled in with whatever is appropriate for the case you are working on. As well as the scriptures that the Lord can have you meditate on may be totally different than these. This example is intended to show you how your encounter could go. The LORD Himself can facilitate your courtroom experience according to your specific needs. The key elements are identifying the lies that need to be countered with scripture and identifying behavior patterns that need to be removed *at the root.*

Have Jesus take you to the Court of Heaven

See the courtroom. *El Shaphat,* Judge of All at the Justice Seat. You are standing with Jesus, your Advocate on the right side of the Courtroom and you also see yourself standing with Satan on the left side of the courtroom. There is an aisle dividing the sides of the courtroom.

There is a large blank screen on the wall and there are many angels present, dressed in white and gold.

The Testimony

(In this example, we are not calling other witnesses to the stand, but this can happen in cases where you are working out issues of relationship conflicts and forgiveness)

The Prosecution

You hear the enemy presenting his case of the words and actions which gave him the contract to mess with you. As proof of his claims, A screen begins to play snippets of your life choices. And you see and hear yourself speaking and behaving in ways that would not honor God. You see and hear yourself speaking limiting and negative lies that go against the truth of your power and identity in scripture. These lies go against your true identity as a Child of God. You see yourself doing and saying things for which you know God has not called you to say and do. These are words and deeds that affect your life and health negatively. You hear Satan defend his rights according to the contract you entered into by these words and actions that permitted him to spiritually attack you.

The enemy rests his case. It is time for the God of Justice to hear the Christ/You side of the case.

Your Defense

Jesus is with you, but He is also covering you. When you speak, He is also speaking. You are speaking as ONE!

SPEAK THE FOLLOWING OUT LOUD TOGETHER---SEEING YOU AND JESUS AS ONE

FATHER, Your word declares that I can come boldly before Your throne of grace, where I can find mercy and grace to help in my time of need. Thank You, Lord, that today I have come humbly before Your throne in reverent honor to make petitions and requests concerning matters where I need Your DIVINE intervention. (Hebrews 4:16)

FATHER, I confess and repent of my sins and the sins of my ancestors where I learned to listen to the enemy's voice over your voice, inviting fear, pride, anxiety, and worry to influence and rule my life. I forgive my ancestors, I forgive myself and I forgive you, God for allowing it to happen to me.

Your Word instructs me to always keep my eyes fixed on You, the Author and Perfector of my faith. (Hebrews 12:2) Therefore, I repent for all disobedience in which I chose to keep my eyes on my circumstances and listened to the lying and limiting the voice of the enemy and acknowledge that these choices blocked Your blessings in my life. Father, I ask that You break every legal contract that the enemy has because of this disobedience that prevents me from walking in the fullness of my God-ordained destiny. I thank You for forgiving me of my sins. I thank You Father for redeeming me from every legal curse.

FATHER, I ask by the authority I have as a Child of the LIVING GOD, that You grant me a full PARDON from the penalty, reproach, and consequences of these sins based upon Jesus' finished work and sacrifice on the cross. Father, I stand on (Romans 8:28-35) and ask You LORD to cleanse me from all unrighteousness.

(Visualize this as you say it) Lord, I praise Your name, for I am free from every form of collective captivity in my family line. Please remove those things from my life that would hinder my fruitfulness. Uproot those things in my life that are not like You. If need be, please show me how I need to release anything further that hinders your best plans for me. (Look and do what He shows you to do)

Father, help me as my natural new and healed heart posture to seek Your face FIRST, and to discover and recover the hidden treasures that You intended for me. Father, walk me back to the foundations of my life and heal, deliver, and redeem me. Rip out from the root of this tendency in my heart to fall into this sin and throw it forever in the sea of forgetfulness. (VISUALIZE THIS AND WATCH WHAT HE DOES) Please restore me to Your original design, and purpose as if the enemy never interfered with my life. (Joel 2:25-32)

Father, as I stand before You, I honor You as the Great Judge of all the earth. I thank You for the Blood of Jesus that is speaking for me according to (Hebrews 12:24). If there are those who can accuse me of anything, Lord, I ask that You not listen to the voice of my accusers but wash me with the Blood of Jesus and make me what You want me to be. (See the Blood of Jesus in the courtroom covering and purifying everything that is not God's will) I thank You that the Blood of Jesus silences every accusation against me. I declare my agreement that can overcome the BLOOD of JESUS!

The Verdict

El Shaphat speaks... According to (Colossians 2:14) I declare that all the written ordinances that would speak against you are now silenced by the Blood of Jesus. that this case in the spirit realm is CLOSED. **Walk in victory** without accusation because you have confessed and repented of these ungodly behaviors and prayed in the Mighty Name and Authority of Jesus Christ.

Thank the Lord and praise Him for His mercy. (Visualize your newly healed heart... What does it look like now?) Purpose in your spirit to walk out this new victory by the power of the Holy Spirit.

Celebrate with Jesus! (Do something incredibly fun with Him in celebration!)

About Dr. Patty Sadallah

Patty Sadallah has a Doctorate of Ministry in Christian Leadership/Discipleship from Christian Leadership University. She is passionate about showing people how to encounter God personally so they may live their lives through faith in Jesus through the power of the Holy Spirit. Her mission is to bring the message of the realness of God and the practicality of intimacy and relationship with God to the masses by incorporating media in her messages.

Dr. Patty is a Professor at Christian Leadership University serving master's and doctoral students. Additionally, she leads the Spirit Life Circle mentored coaching ministry offered internationally through Communion with God Ministries.

She has more than 35 years of experience serving faith-based nonprofit organizations and small groups as an Organization Development Consultant, Coach, Facilitator, Trainer, and Bible Study Leader.

She is the Leader of the Spirit Life Workshops Ministry leading full weekend workshops that draw you closer to God and equip you for your Christ Identity callings. Check out https://SpiritLifeWorkshops. com for the latest workshop opportunity.

Dr. Patty would love to create a custom-designed workshop or be a Speaker or Keynote for your conference or ministry event. Contact her at Patty@SpiritLifeWorkshops.com to discuss those options.

Patty and George have been married since 1986 and have three lovely daughters: Jamael, Leah, and Noelle. Jamael and her husband Nick have their sweet grandchildren.

Books by Dr. Patty Sadallah

r. Patty Sadallah has authored the award-winning *Clips that Move Mountains 2nd Edition*, a Discipleship book that includes 23 film clips, and *Journey to the Abundant Christian Life*, its Bible study companion.

Additionally, *How to Live a Worry-Free Life: Just Ask Jesus Book 1.* Look for more in this series after the completion of the Experience Jesus series.

The **Experience Jesus Series** includes 4 books and each has or will have an accompanying Experience Journal that includes topical scriptures on each journal page and several more journal prompts for discussion and encounters. Each journal prompt provides more opportunities to get to know every featured name in each book.

Book 1: *How to Encounter the LOVE of God*

Book 2: *How to Encounter the HEALING of God*

Book 3: *How to Encounter the DIRECTION of God*

Book 4: *How to Encounter the POWER of God*

You can find all books, journals, and downloadable resources at Dr. Patty's online bookstore at https://PattySadallah.com/shop.

If you are outside of the US, you can still find Dr. Patty's books on **Amazon.com** and **BarnesAndNoble.com** The easiest way to find Dr. Sadallah's books is to **simply search "Patty Sadallah"** on these bookstore websites.

Check out more about each book and the other ministry opportunities by visiting her website at **www.PattySadallah.com**

Dr. Patty is available for speaking, teaching, and facilitation related to discipleship for individuals, small groups, organizations, and multi-organizational planning needs.

Check out her Spirit Life Workshops ministry at https://SpiritLifeWorkshops.com for live events that teach you how to grow in Christ and live out your Christ Identity!

www.ingramcontent.com/pod-product-compliance
Lightning Source LLC
Chambersburg PA
CBHW060914120626
46553CB00001B/318